"In *Redeeming Sex*, Deb Hirsch helps the church catch a vision of relationship that can lead to love and life where now there is often confusion and pain. . . . I appreciate her openness and honesty as hard questions around gender and sexuality are explored from a place of love and a desire for holy intimacy."

Bruxy Cavey, teaching pastor at the Meeting House, author of *The End of Religion*

"The beautiful heart of *Redeeming Sex* i⌐
Jesus is the embodiment of sexuality ar
our model for right living and right lo
rative, witty and earthy language, an(
Hirsch encourages readers to connect
dimension of life—with the life of Chriɛ

Jenell Paris, Messiah College, author of *The End of Sexual Identity*

"What the homosexuality debate needs is convincing testimony. That's what *Redeeming Sex* offers: Debra Hirsch's own story—and what she learned about sex before and after meeting Jesus—is both convincing and convicting. But the book is more than testimony. . . . It can lead Christians to an integration of sex and sanctity that makes us more faithful and redemptive disciples of Jesus Christ."

Howard A. Snyder, author of *Homosexuality and the Church*

"Finally. A thoughtful, biblical, yet paradigm-busting discussion on the hottest topic in the church and culture today. *Redeeming Sex* pulls no punches yet graciously guides us toward the heart of God in our human sexuality."

Hugh Halter, author of *Flesh*

"Join the conversation about *Redeeming Sex*. Deb takes a challenging conversation and brings humility, authenticity and truth to help us all talk more openly and honestly about this important topic. Thank you, Deb Hirsch!"

Dave Ferguson, lead pastor of Community Christian Church

"This book challenges us to love God and people through the lens of our sexuality. Deb pushes us to see sexuality not as something to be done secretly in closets and dark rooms but as the beauty of God. This book challenges—for sure—but it's a must read."

Leroy Barber, global executive director, Word Made Flesh

"With lived experience, direct frankness and a pastoral heart, Deb Hirsch addresses the church on sexuality. In so doing, *Redeeming Sex* prepares the way for the places the church must go to be 'among' today's confused and strife-ridden world of sexuality. It is a vulnerable gift that moves us beyond faulty stereotypes and pre-set notions. I cannot think of a better book to start the conversation."

David Fitch, Northern Seminary, author of *Prodigal Christianity*

"If you are willing to invest the time to listen—really listen—to what Deb Hirsch is saying about the vexing and complex nature of human sexuality, you won't fail to be moved by her allegiance to radical grace, her trust in the potency of genuine hospitality and her unyielding confidence in the power of God to reconcile, repair and renew us all."

Michael Frost, author of *Incarnate* and *Exiles*

"I can't think of a person I'd rather listen to give us biblical, Jesus-lens insight . . . than my friend Deb Hirsch. I believe this is going to totally connect with the hearts of so many needing to move beyond the usual explanations or ways this discussion normally happens as we rethink, rediscover and redeem sexuality."

Dan Kimball, pastor of Vintage Faith Church, author of *They Like Jesus but Not the Church*

"I'm so grateful to Deb Hirsch for writing the best book on this conversation I have read. It speaks to the heart of our identity in Christ. It addresses complex and sensitive realities and tensions with grace, love, compassion, truth, justice and mercy. It is prophetic, profound, candid, transparent and should be read by every Christian. . . . I am giving a copy of this book to everyone I know. It's that important."

Christine Caine, director, Equip & Empower Ministries

"Deb Hirsch has . . . brought biblical clarity to one of the most misunderstood and controversial topics of the day. Many have either sensationalized or minimized our sexuality, leaving us confused, embarrassed or ashamed about the sexual nature of our humanity. But Deb has taken in this beautiful gift of God and woven it together with a Jesus-centered vision of how sexuality can glorify God and lead us to flourish."

Jon Tyson, author, *Sacred Roots*, founding pastor, Trinity Grace Church, New York

REDEEMING
SEX

NAKED CONVERSATIONS ABOUT
SEXUALITY AND SPIRITUALITY

DEBRA HIRSCH

FOREWORD BY GABE LYONS

IVP Books

An imprint of InterVarsity Press
Downers Grove, Illinois

InterVarsity Press
P.O. Box 1400, Downers Grove, IL 60515-1426
ivpress.com
email@ivpress.com

InterVarsity Press® is the book-publishing division of InterVarsity Christian Fellowship/USA®, a movement of students and faculty active on campus at hundreds of universities, colleges and schools of nursing in the United States of America, and a member movement of the International Fellowship of Evangelical Students. For information about local and regional activities, visit intervarsity.org.

All Scripture quotations, unless otherwise indicated, are taken from THE HOLY BIBLE, NEW INTERNATIONAL VERSION®, NIV® Copyright © 1973, 1978, 1984, 2011 by Biblica, Inc.™ Used by permission. All rights reserved worldwide.

Use of the Kinsey scale courtesy of the Kinsey Institute for Research in Sex, Gender and Reproduction.

While any stories in this book are true, some names and identifying information may have been changed to protect the privacy of individuals.

Cover design: Cindy Kiple
Interior design: Beth McGill
Cover and spine images: SuperStock/Glow Images

ISBN 978-0-8308-3639-0 (print)
ISBN 978-0-8308-9810-7 (digital)

Printed in the United States of America ♾

Library of Congress Cataloging-in-Publication Data
Hirsch, Debra, 1963-
 Redeeming sex : naked conversations about sexuality and spirituality
/ Debra Hirsch.
    pages cm
 Includes bibliographical references.
 ISBN 978-0-8308-3639-0 (pbk. : alk. paper) -- ISBN 978-0-8308-9810-7
(digital)
 1. Sex--Religious aspects--Christianity. I. Title.
 BT708.H57 2015
 233'.5--dc23

                                                            2015006636

P *21* *20* *19* *18* *17* *16* *15* *14* *13* *12* *11* *10* *9* *8* *7* *6* *5*

Y *32* *31* *30* *29* *28* *27* *26* *25* *24* *23* *22* *21* *20* *19*

To Sharon and Mark

Our stories are three, yet one.

From my heart to yours, eternally bonded.

Then I saw a new heaven and a new earth, for the old heaven and the old earth had disappeared. And the sea was also gone. And I saw the holy city, the new Jerusalem, coming down from God out of heaven like a bride beautifully dressed for her husband.

I heard a loud shout from the throne, saying, "Look, God's home is now among his people! He will live with them, and they will be his people. God himself will be with them. He will wipe every tear from their eyes, and there will be no more death or sorrow or crying or pain. All these things are gone forever."

And the one sitting on the throne said, "Look, I am making everything new!" . . . And he also said, "It is finished! I am the Alpha and the Omega—the Beginning and the End. To all who are thirsty I will give freely from the springs of the water of life. All who are victorious will inherit all these blessings, and I will be their God, and they will be my children."—Rev 21:1-7 NLT

Contents

Foreword

Until now, few books have articulately expressed a grounded, holistic, nuanced, intellectually honest and loving approach to sexuality. Debra places this conversation in its proper place, moving us away from the "gay issue" to properly deal with the broader questions it raises around our sexuality, intimacy and the church's role in sustaining relationships.

Debra explicitly shares her personal journey. Writing in a nonprescriptive and nonjudgmental way, Debra rouses our curiosity to consider a deeper way to think about our sexuality. In a culture obsessed with sexual expression, orientations and gender identity, she helps properly order the role these things should play in our lives.

Debra's humility and candor make this topic approachable, even fun. I don't know that I've read a book with more appropriate references to orgasm, with raw honesty about our sexual appetites and their relationship to our spirituality. At first you might feel awkward, but then you'll find it refreshing.

But more than Debra's authentic writing style, her curation of knowledge and depth of experience on the topics at hand are a godsend in our age. We couldn't have a better guide than Debra Hirsch leading us forward.

Conversations about sexuality can feel risky. Reflecting on the dynamics at play, I picture a treacherous path winding up the face of a rocky, stone-faced cliff. Our self-preserving questions and a fear of the unknown may hold us back. We wonder

What if I take the wrong step?

What if this costs me my reputation?

What if I fail?

These questions and fears understandably keep many people flat-footed on the ground. We've watched the casualties of those who dared to go before us. We've learned from their mistakes that every step matters, placing our grip on the wrong protruding rock can result in utter devastation, and the risks are enormous. Though the path is narrow, deep down we know it's one we must ascend. Faithfulness demands we engage the issue of our day with the weight and seriousness it requires.

While some tire of the conversation, I urge you to press on. We sit at the beginning of a moment that will not soon go away. Make no mistake, you will be asked the question. And because you invested the time to read this book, your answer will be full of grace, mercy, truth and clarity—something your friends and family long for, but few have found. I pray you find it in the pages of this book.

Gabe Lyons

Introduction

Foreplay

A human being is nothing but a story with skin around it.

FRED ALLEN

George was my drug dealer. He was also the sound engineer in a band I hung out with. All in all he was a pretty wild character who in his calmer moments saw himself as a seeker, a philosopher of sorts, in that he would get stoned, stare at the stars, and get all deep and spiritual.

I didn't take George's seeking all that seriously given that his pursuit of truth didn't extend to his drug dealing or ripping off his friends. George got picked up by the police for a stack of unpaid parking fines and was sentenced to two weeks in the local jail. Keeping on with his quest for truth (and to quell some of the boredom), he took along his mother's big Greek Orthodox family Bible. I can't imagine what the police thought when he walked in with it. It probably weighed ten pounds.

You know what happens next. George begins reading that big Bible and the Holy Spirit falls on him. He is born again right there in the local lockup!

When the police released George ten days later, he was bursting at the seams—ready to tell the world about his newfound faith. His brother John picked him up from jail and gave his life to Christ before they even arrived home.

The two then banded together, Bibles under one arm and a copy of Hal Lindsey's *The Late Great Planet Earth* under the other (it was the 1980s after all!), and went out in hot pursuit of new converts. They compiled a list of all the people they sold drugs to and called it their evangelistic "hit list." They would pray for each person and then catch up with them to tell them about Jesus. I was on this hit list, as were a number of my friends, including my sister Sharon and dearest friend Mark, the two to whom this book is dedicated.

My journey of faith didn't actually begin when George shared the gospel with me; God had been working my case for a long time. I just hadn't realized it. Like George, I was a seeker, and in the weeks before coming to Jesus I had sensed something was in the wind. I kept telling my friend Jason that my "answer" was just around the corner. He thought I was taking too many drugs, and maybe I was. But I was expectant, never thinking for a moment that my answer, like George's, would also be Jesus.

When Jesus came into my life everything changed. All those old clichés you hear—being lost and then found, being blind and then seeing—applied to me. I encountered God in such a dramatic way that I knew my life would never be the same. Within a very short time both Sharon and Mark also gave their lives to Jesus. The three of us were living with a bunch of others in a big community house, and were living and identifying as gay.

God set up residence among a group of people who had little clue about him or what the journey of faith entails. Within a period of about six months over fifty people—friends and contacts—had come to know Jesus. But not everyone who lived with us was thrilled about our newfound faith. There was much debate and sometimes outright hostility. At times it felt like the two kingdoms were warring against one another. And they were! But God's Spirit was at work, and a new community of Jesus followers was being formed. Originally intended to indulge our hedonistic lifestyles, our home became a place for all sorts of people seeking refuge, healing and personal transformation.

A FATEFUL PRAYER MEETING

But we didn't have a church. George had found God in prison; we had no real connection with other believers in the outside world. As I look back now, I laugh thinking how easily we could have ended up as some weird cult. But intuitively we knew we needed to go to church and meet other Christians.

One night Sharon and Mark stumbled on a cute, old church building with the name "Christian Chapel" above the doors. Seeing a light shining from a side room, they knocked tentatively on the door. An older, willowy-looking man appeared. He was dressed in a white shirt and tie and introduced himself as Pat, the pastor of the church. Pat explained that they were in the middle of a prayer meeting and invited Sharon and Mark to join. They nervously declined but said they would be back Sunday morning with their friends.

A few days later about twelve of us trundled along to the church. As we made our way down the center aisle to the front of that little Christian Chapel, I'm not sure who was more shocked, the church members or us. Talk about a clash of cultures. The men were wearing suits, and the ladies had on hats and gloves. We were dressed like we had just rolled out of bed after a hard night of partying. I still had on my pajama top!

We were a ragtag bunch of ex-prostitutes, drug dealers, gays, punks and goths. They were a fundamentalist church filled with conservative-looking old folk. Yet despite the obvious differences between us and them, we managed to stay. Those older folk had no clue what to do with us, but they did know how to love and how to pray. They somehow managed to reach across the cultural divide to lovingly embrace us and include us in the bigger church family. The early years of our discipleship were worked out in the context of that little church.

Not all those church folk embraced us that easily, of course. There was some grumbling going on behind the scenes. Pat eventually let us in on a little secret: given that the "youth" group was in their sixties, that Wednesday night prayer meeting that Sharon and Mark stumbled on had been set up specifically to pray that God would bring young people into their church. Pat would constantly remind the grumblers that *we* were the answer to their prayers, and it wasn't his fault they weren't specific enough with God about the type of young people they wanted!

Pat really was one amazing, grace-filled pastor; it was like nothing fazed him. He came to our home dressed in his suit and tie every Wednesday to lead a Bible study. Nothing too radical about that, except that while the Bible was being taught around our kitchen table, drugs just might be being bought and sold in the living room, men could be in bed with each other upstairs, and it was highly likely the crazy Greek brothers John and George would be noisily casting out demons in the backyard!

Pat used to tell us we were the apples of his eye. He never once took a moralistic, tongue-clucking approach with us. He knew God was at work in us, and he didn't want to mess with that. He knew the Holy Spirit would eventually sort some things out, and despite how he might have personally felt about our crazy lifestyles and wild household, he remained true. I can still see him sitting at our table with his big Scofield Bible and that little twinkle in his eye. And while he did eventually ditch his suit coat, he always wore his characteristic shirt and tie.

Many of us eventually left the Christian Chapel to go into fulltime ministry—a wonderful testament to a church that was willing to go beyond their own comfort zones to embrace a strange people from a strange land.

In many ways Pat embodies the thesis of this book. His ability to see the bigger picture of God's redemptive purpose and priorities meant he didn't get judgmental or controlling, nor did he push us beyond what we were ready to own and live. He modeled Jesus in his open-hearted posture toward those who were seen as sexually scandalous—a posture that is sorely needed within the church in any time and place.

FREAK CHURCH

I met my husband, Alan, in those early years. He became the leader of a small group we ran in that community house, and we instantly became friends. He, Mark and I all ended up going to the same seminary. Moving from a house full of weird and wonderful people into a conservative Christian college was like stepping into another, even stranger, world. But despite some major cultural clashes, we survived and soaked in our time learning about God's Word and our newfound faith.

After seminary Al and I were married by Pat. He helped us transition into our first formal ministry role, a church located in an inner city suburb of Melbourne, Australia. Many of our friends came with us to South Melbourne Restoration Community (affectionately called "South"), which caused the church to double in size overnight. We soon became known as something of a "freak" church—a haven for people who didn't fit in at regular churches.

Among those drawn to South were a number of LGBT folk, averaging at least a quarter of our community at any given point in time. Given this, we regularly sought help to make sense of what discipleship looked like for LGBT people. You'll find some of these stories laced throughout the book.

Along the way we also collected a good dose of disillusioned Christians—some barely hanging on to their faith. Someone once said of "South" that God had positioned us two hundred feet away from hell—a place for those on their way to or struggling with faith, and the last stop for those on their way out. If people couldn't survive Christianity with us, then they couldn't survive it anywhere! "South" lived the raw stuff of the gospel. With Jesus firmly at our center, we had an open-table policy—*all* the weird and wonderful were welcome. Our experience taught us that most people needed to feel a sense of *belonging* before they believed. And they needed *acceptance* before they could even begin to understand what repentance or transformation might look like. When you invite the messiness of broken humanity, you also invite amazing grace.

Al and I had the privilege of leading this unique community for over sixteen years, and we loved every minute of it. "South" was a community that didn't flinch or shock too easily; we saw sexuality as simply part and parcel of being human, of being a disciple. And while sexuality certainly can be scandalous, we realized that there is nothing too shocking for God. Sexuality was God's idea in the first place; he not only understands it but knows the type of power it can wield over us. And he understands how it causes us to stumble again and again. God gets it.

If our sexuality lies close to our spirituality, as I suggest it does, then it's vital we find a way to bring a living, holy sexuality back into the context of the church. How can any of us be real, authentic people if we have to leave our sexuality at the door? And how can we speak to a sexually confused world if we have nothing to say?

This book really is a summation of my life's experience, my own encounter with Jesus and my full-time immersion in ministry for over twenty-five years now. I have led churches in both Australia and Los Angeles, and worked in the field of sexuality for as many years. I write this book first and foremost as a disciple of Jesus, a ministry practitioner, a missionary and a lover of people. While I am a trained counselor and ordained minister of the gospel, I am neither a trained ethicist nor a professional theologian. The reader will find here a combination of insights from theology, psychology and other social sciences.

Redeeming Sex is not a systematic theology or a methodical psychology, so please don't look for these. It is much more of a testimony and a challenge to the church in a critical time when sexuality is being negotiated—in the church and out. The seed of this book was penned in a chapter of *Untamed*, an award-winning book about discipleship and mission that I wrote with my husband. Please take a look at that to frame these issues in the much broader context of what it means to be an untamed disciple of Jesus.[1]

Throughout the book you will find me pointing us toward a much more redemptive understanding of sexuality than the one we ordinarily have. By this I mean that we need to move beyond the largely moralistic, disgraced, traditional dualistic suppression of the body (and the soul, for that matter) that has marked Christianity in the Western tradition. We need to (re)apply to our sexualities the radical grace and salvation that we all must find in Jesus. We must apply this to ourselves and also to our neighbors and society at large. And while I tend to hang out on the more traditional side of Christian sexual ethics, you might be surprised at just how "unconventional" this can look when one follows in the radical way of Jesus.

I want to assure you of my deep, personal participation in the material I humbly lay before you. It is never my intention to overwhelm you or even to necessarily convince you of the rightness of my theological opinion. This book is about the *posture* one takes, not the *position* one holds. I *do* however want to be your conversation partner. So converse with me. Please give me space and grace to be myself—an all-too-human woman who is trying to work this all out on behalf of my Lord and my friends and the mission of the church. I do love God and his people, and want us all to get this right.

Finally, while, for the most part, I have learned about sexuality through my own and other's experiences, the opinions and beliefs in this book *are entirely mine* and do not necessarily reflect those of family, friends or my current faith community (Tribe of Los Angeles). Although they all form part of my story, they are not responsible for my narrative.

*The reward of the search is to go on searching.
The soul's desire is fulfilled by the very fact of its
remaining unsatisfied, for really to see God is
never to have had one's fill of desiring Him.*

GREGORY OF NYSSA

Part One

WHERE DID ALL THE SEXY CHRISTIANS GO?

Oh My God!

Sexuality Meets Spirituality

*The only thing wrong with being an atheist is that
there's nobody to talk to during an orgasm.*

AUTHOR UNKNOWN

*The sexual confusion so prevalent in our world and
in our own hearts is simply the human desire
for heaven gone berserk.*

CHRISTOPHER WEST

Imagine if heaven was like one endless orgasm. That's what my husband thinks.

We were having a conversation about sexuality (nothing new in our home), and I was commenting on the temporal nature of the orgasm, how overrated it is in our culture, and what role, if any, it would play in heaven. It was then that my mischievous husband suggested we wouldn't need orgasms in heaven: heaven would be like one endless orgasm. We both laughed, but as we continued talking, it dawned on us that there was more truth in it than we first realized.

Orgasms are one of the most sought-after experiences in life—which is strange, because it's not like they last forever or even a few weeks, like a long-anticipated holiday. We're talking about something that is over within seconds. That isn't to say that getting to that moment isn't part of the allure; it is, but it's the climax that we are really seeking. Those final few moments are so filled with such ecstasy and pleasure that for a moment nothing else in the world seems to matter.

Anything that feels *that* good is just begging to be repeated, which is perhaps precisely why our culture seems to be so fixated with sex. The distorting allure of pornography aside, thousands of books and magazines are published every year teaching us how to be better lovers, how to understand our pleasure zones, showing us a myriad of ways we can experiment sexually—all designed to help us enhance our orgasmic experience.

Is that why sex is so alluring to the human race? Are we simply creatures bent on pleasurable experiences? Is the orgasm the carrot on an evolutionary stick, rewarding our biologically innate drive to procreate? Or is there something more going on? Is there something *else* that calls to us within those brief moments of ecstasy? Something of a more primal nature, a deeper experience that helps us rise above the banality of our day-to-day lives?

Time magazine, hardly a theological journal, raised the same questions back in 2004—suggesting there is more to our pursuit of sex than just, well, brute sex:

> Of all the splendidly ridiculous, transcendently fulfilling things humans do, it's sex—with its countless permutations of practices and partners—that most confounds understanding. What in the world are we doing? Why in the world are we so consumed by it? The impulse to procreate may lie at the heart of sex, but like the impulse to nourish ourselves, it is merely the starting point for an astonishingly varied banquet. Bursting

from our sexual center is a whole spangle of other things—art, song, romance, obsession, rapture, sorrow, companionship, love, even violence and criminality—all playing an enormous role in everything from our physical health to our emotional health to our politics, our communities, our very life spans.

Why should this be so? Did nature simply overload us in the mating department, hot-wiring us for the sex that is so central to the survival of the species, and never mind the sometimes sloppy consequences? Or is there something smarter and subtler at work, some larger interplay among sexuality, life and what it means to be human?[1]

I believe that within both the desire and the pleasure of sex are found deeper human longings for *eternal* connection and ecstasy. There is, in other words, something deeply spiritual about sex.

I'm not just talking about the orgasm here, but every aspect of our sexuality: our capacity for relationships, our longing for love, our identity as male and female, all point to something beyond oneself, to the "Eternal Other." I have come to believe that our sexuality is so interlaced with longing for and experience of spirituality that we cannot access one without somehow tapping into the other.

SPARKS OF ETERNITY

The late psychiatrist M. Scott Peck was convinced that buried in our explicit pursuit of sex is an implicit pursuit of God. He noted that sex is likely to be the closest that most people ever come to a genuine spiritual experience. It was this yearning for the spiritual, he contended, that explained why so many chase after sex with a repetitive, desperate kind of abandon. "It is no accident," he wrote, "that even atheists and agnostics will, at the moment of orgasm, routinely cry out, 'Oh God!'"[2]

Rabbi Shmuley Boteach, in his wonderfully refreshing book *Kosher Sex*, also highlights this transcendent appeal of sex:

In lovemaking our ultimate objective is to transcend the body. We experience an intense pleasure that makes us feel really good about our partner, the object of our love. We have an out-of-body experience. We feel transported by the sexual encounter, lifted above the constraints of the body and meeting at the level of the soul. This is what orgasm is all about. It is an intensely unifying moment in which a man and a woman experience a spiritual epiphany.[3]

Even the meaning of the term *ecstasy* (*ek-stasis*) implies something "outside of oneself," which is suggestive of the often-reported loss of ego awareness and personal boundaries we experience in orgasm. Will there be sex in heaven? Christopher West comes close to full agreement with my husband's cheeky statement: "The union of the sexes as we know it now will give way to an *infinitely greater* Union. Those who are raised in glory will experience bliss so far superior to earthly sexual union that our wee brains can't even begin to imagine it."[4]

Think about the sense of freedom or liberation that is captured even within just a few moments, when one is seemingly transported into a different realm—one free from the worries and concerns of complicated lives and the limitations of physical bodies. Orgasms offer us fleeting experiences of transcendence, a way of losing ourselves, a mechanism to find and experience the "other." Such ecstasy has always played a role in all forms of mysticism and worship, and these in turn anticipate a final consummation, suggesting a place or state where we will finally experience ultimate and eternal freedom.

I can clearly remember a young guy confessing to me that the only time he truly felt free was when he experienced an orgasm, which was why he felt driven to repeat them again and again—often multiple times a day! He was clearly exhibiting addictive behavior, but isn't such freedom and transcendence as that embedded in the orgasm an intrinsic part of any addiction? Are not all our vices virtues gone wrong? Is there not, in all our addictive behavior, something deeper being sought?

Without wanting to simplify the complex psychology and motivations behind addictive behaviors, it's not hard to see a perverse spirituality at work in them. G. K. Chesterton was on cue when he suggested that a man knocking on the door of a brothel is in fact looking for God. We all often look for the right things (connection, ecstasy, touch, yearning to be known, etc.) in the wrong places.

Many Eastern religious traditions have, in fact, been on about this for centuries, claiming that our moments of ecstasy are never just about bodily pleasure and connection, but are actually filled with spiritual significance. Some talk about being elevated "spiritually" in ecstatic moments, likening them to a moment of nirvana—a kind of temporary oneness with the universe. Osho, an Indian mystic and professor of philosophy, saw the orgasm as a mini-*samadhi* (achieved when one has love of God). These can transport us into a state of rapture where the ego disappears and we step outside of time into the timeless—a "now" of bliss.[5]

The French have an interesting little phrase that I think also captures something of this. The moments after orgasm are called *la petite mort*, "a little death," a reference to the expenditure of one's "life force."[6] These moments elicit feelings of transcendence and, for some, melancholy. I know of people who habitually cry after reaching orgasm, demonstrating that sex can be experienced as invoking a nascent sense of pain and loss. The famous literary critic Roland Barthes spoke of *la petite mort* as why people read great literature—it gives the reader a feeling of transcendence, liberation and release.

Whatever it is that one is seeking in sex, one thing seems clear—it's more than just about momentary pleasure, as intoxicating as that can be. It seems that almost all the existential and religious aspects of human life are somehow mysteriously involved.

Sex then isn't just about sex. And maybe this *is* one of the reasons our culture is so fixated with sex—because in it they are also looking for "something else." And just so that we don't miss the point, this innate *spirituality* of sex isn't just limited to the fleeting orgasm or to the intensely intimate act of sex itself. The whole allure of sexuality and the associated desire to overcome loneliness through relational connection seem to point to far deeper human longings to *know* and *be known*, not just by one another but supremely by the "Other."

TWO SIDES OF THE ONE COIN

Perhaps at this stage it would be helpful to take a closer look at how I define both spirituality and sexuality. These definitions will apply for the course of this book.

Spirituality can be described as a vast longing that drives us beyond ourselves in an attempt to connect with, to probe and to understand our world. And beyond that, it is the inner compulsion to connect with the Eternal Other, which is God. Essentially, it is *a longing to know and be known by God (on physical, emotional, psychological and spiritual levels).* This is why we are called to worship God with all that we are—body, mind and soul (Deuteronomy 6:4-9; Mark 12:29-31).

Sexuality can be described as the deep desire and longing that drives us beyond ourselves in an attempt to connect with, to understand, that which is other than ourselves. Essentially, it is *a longing to know and be known by other people (on physical, emotional, psychological and spiritual levels).*[7] It thus forms part of what it means to "love others as we love ourselves" (Mark 12:29-31).

Defined in these ways the similarities become obvious. It turns out that sexuality and spirituality are in fact two sides of the same coin. Both express a deep longing to know and be known—by God and by others. Both involve a call to learn the true meaning and practice of love. And isn't this exactly how God created us—with both spiritual and sexual longings?

Both of these yearnings are essential to what it means to be human. Our deepest longings as human beings are to be in relationship with God and our neighbor—this really and simply *is* the human condition. The Hebrew word *yada* ("to know") is, in fact, used for both sexual intercourse as well as our relationship with God.[8]

Yada implies contact, intimacy and relation. It refers both to sexual intimacy in the narrowest sense of the word (in Adam *knowing* Eve) but also to our knowledge of God. This is significant: to *yada* God doesn't mean just having some abstract theoretical knowledge *about* God, but rather being *connected to* God. It implies an intimate and distinctly *experiential* knowledge *of* God, a direct encounter with the holy. And so whether we wish to point to the fullness of sexuality (knowing others) or the fullness of our spirituality (knowing God), *yada* is the word we're searching for.[9]

> Every relational event is a stage that affords one a glimpse into the consummating event.
>
> **Martin Buber**

KNOW GOD, NO SEX?

Despite what now appears to me to be the overwhelmingly obvious connections between spirituality and sexuality, when I first came to faith and went to church, I had the sneaking suspicion that God had nothing to do with sex—well, apart from the fact that he didn't want single people doing it. Sex was clearly only for married people. Church seemed so sexless to me that I wasn't even convinced married people were doing it, except that they kept having kids!

By that point in my life, talking about sex, having sex, even experimenting sexually was a pretty normal part of life. When I went to church, then, it was like being time warped back into my grandmother's era, where sex was off-limits, both in word and in deed. "Having" sex was something you did as infrequently as possible, in hushed whispers, under covers with the lights off.

This sex-as-taboo culture was a real problem for me and the others I came to faith with. We had a thousand questions and a church full of people not willing, or even able, to talk about it. And when sex did come up (in gender-specific Bible studies), it always seemed to be from the negative—that is, what Christians were *not allowed* to do. There was little connection to the grander themes of spirituality, or understanding from a psychological perspective— just rules and regulations about what we do and don't do with our "bits and bobs." Moreover, we were constantly being warned that the enemy was "prowling around like a roaring lion" looking for any opportunity to tempt us—always sexually, oddly enough. I was left with the distinct feeling that God had abandoned all things sexual to the playground of the devil.

It's funny because now I can't even read the Bible without noticing the sexual language and imagery laced all throughout Scripture.

- Israel is described as God's lover and wife (Ezekiel 16:8; Jeremiah 3:14).

- Unfaithful Israel as the unfaithful wife is accused of "spreading her legs" to foreign gods (Ezekiel 16:15-34; Jeremiah 3:1-3; 31:32; Hosea 2:2-5).

- The church is called the bride of Christ and will finally be joined together with her husband (the final consummation) at the marriage supper of the Lamb (2 Corinthians 11:2; Ephesians 5:25-27; Revelation 19:7-9).

- The Song of Songs is one deeply erotic book, from chapter one all the way to chapter eight.

And what of circumcision? A mark on the penis operates as the sign of God's covenant with his people; the most sensitive part of the male body, where he consummates his most intimate relationships. And the very appendage by which men might be unfaithful in their relationships becomes a daily reminder to covenant obligations and worship. We are also encouraged to receive with meekness the implanted seed of the Word of God (James 1:21), an image that invites us to allow God to actually impregnate us. Use your imagination! And these are but a few.

GOD HINTING

James Nelson describes sexuality as the central clue to what God is up to in the world.[10] While this might seem a little over the top, when you think about it, sexuality factors integrally in our relationships, and relationships *are* what life is all about. At the very least, none of us would be here if people didn't have sex—not just our parents but all the generations before them. It seems our sexual longings show us that God has designed us for sociability, relationships, love and intimacy. When God said that it is not good for people to be alone (Genesis 2:18), he meant it.

There really is no avoiding it: the human race simply wouldn't exist without sexuality, and neither would there be the possibility of community or civil society. Our sexuality drives us out of isolation and into the world of people, and ultimately into fruitful and fulfilling relationships. Sexuality is so central to who we are and what we are about in the world that it is actually impossible to unravel it from our humanity without it all coming undone. Sex seems to be coded into life itself. And not just human life either—"birds do it, bees do it, even educated fleas do it."[11] Yet human life is different. We are set apart from the rest of creation, given a special mark, the very mark of God. Our sexuality needs to be understood in light of this.

If we are created in the image of God, then our sexuality reflects something of who God is. Sex is not just a means to the end of the propagation of the species, or even for fun, but to make the Creator known.

If sex is one of the prime things that God is up to in our world, then Christopher West is spot on when he says that "the way we understand and express our sexuality points to our deepest-held convictions about who we are, who God is, the meaning of love, the ordering of society, and even the ordering of the universe."[12] How we understand and live out our sexuality is profoundly important because we will either reflect our Creator or not.

So when it comes to sexuality we must take our cues from God—
who not only designed us sexually but guides us to its very best
expression.

Fortunately, wonderfully, our sexuality forever points us toward
our Creator—especially when expressed in healthy, "right" ways,
but even in its brokenness, because this is when we become acutely
aware of a deeper longing.

SEX IS A SIGNPOST

In his wonderful book *Simply Christian*, N. T. Wright talks about
four areas within human experience that echo something beyond the
temporal. He describes them as "signposts pointing beyond the landscape of our contemporary culture," and when interpreted correctly
they can lead people into an encounter with God.[13] One of these is
our sexuality, and by extension our capacity for relationships.

> The whole area of human relationships forms another "echo
> of a voice"—an echo which we can ignore if we choose to do
> so, but which is loud enough to get through the defenses of
> a good many people within the supposedly secular world. Or
> if you prefer, human relationships are another signpost
> pointing away into a mist, telling us that there is a road ahead
> which leads to . . . well, which leads somewhere we might
> want to go.[14]

Properly understood and expressed, our sexuality can be an
amazing access point for people to rediscover God. Our personhood
and capacity for relationship are what make us human—and also
Godlike. Contained within these attributes is an inherent yearning
for God. Our sexuality is the stuff of passion and of pain. It is what
pushes us outside of ourselves into the fearful but wonderful world
of relationships. It's the desire within us to *know* and *be known*, to
love and *be loved*—the stuff of the heart of intimacy. And even
though we only experience it as broken beings, it is still the very

thing that points humanity toward its Creator. Jim Cotter captures this beautifully: "There is always a beyondness that seems to beckon in and through our sexuality and sexual relationships, and sex never yields all that it promises of creativity and communion."[15]

It is the brokenness and temporary nature of our sexuality that creates the hunger for the complete and the perfect. And what human being on the planet doesn't experience this! Sexuality and all that goes with it, including both its pleasure and pain, are common to all humanity. We all feel its pull, we experience its joys, we suffer its pains, and we also know its terrible compulsions. We fear both its capacity for darkness and even its power to liberate. And in its expression, both the good and bad, we are able to identify with other people. Acknowledging our own broken sexuality enables us to identify with a sexually broken humanity.

Our sexuality is indeed a powerful force. It can lead us to something of an experience of either heaven or hell, depending on our ability to orient it toward God or not. This is why it not only needs to be understood and integrated into our spirituality, but also handled with great care—and why it's imperative for Christians to talk more openly about it.

Modesty Gone Mad

Life in Lubbock, Texas, taught me two things: One is that God loves you and you're going to burn in hell. The other is that sex is the most awful, filthy thing on earth, and you should save it for someone you love.

BUTCH HANCOCK

Back in the late 1990s, our church in Melbourne hosted a conference on sexuality and spirituality. We invited our good friend Michael Frost to be the keynote speaker and to speak on issues contained in his then recently released book *Longing for Love*. In preparation for the event I went to our local Christian bookstore to order several cases of the book. I couldn't find any on the shelf, so I asked one of the staff if they had any left in stock. She informed me that management insisted the books be kept in a box under the counter. They were too risqué to be seen on display. I wish I could show you the cover so you could see how unrisqué it really is. It simply showed a man and woman in an embrace; the only nakedness you saw was one part of the woman's back. Both the man and woman were even wearing wedding rings. It was hardly sexy! Even most toothpaste ads on billboards are likely to have more raw sex appeal.

I drove away from the bookshop completely stunned. *Surely Christians are not this bound up! What are we thinking? That someone is going to masturbate over the cover? Seriously?*

More importantly for the topic of this book, what understanding of sexuality is being expressed in this mindset?

Twenty years later and one might be excused for thinking that little has changed. The example that quickly comes to mind is the controversy around a female author wanting to use the word *vagina* in her upcoming book. Is there something wrong with this or is it just me? The fact is that more than half the population actually do have vaginas! And it was God himself who designed and created them! And what about all the restrictive and somewhat arbitrary boundaries imposed on men and women in cross-gender friend-ships? Surely we can do better than this.

THE NOT-SO-SEXY CHURCH

I don't know about you, but when I think of someone as being sexual or sexy, I don't usually think of church folk. In all likelihood I'm thinking of Marilyn Monroe, Madonna or Brad Pitt. I'm probably not thinking of Billy Graham!

Why the disconnect? If spirituality and sexuality are as intricately linked as I'm suggesting, then one would think that the spiritual people would be some of the sexiest people on the planet! Clearly this doesn't appear to be the case!

But make no mistake, whether we like it or not, sexuality con-tinues to define much of who we are. It is alive and well, evidenced in the inordinate negative attention we give it in attitudes, behaviors and our incessant need to both control and regulate it. We might not talk, integrate or understand it very well, but we certainly have a relationship with it—it's just not always the most healthy.

Even our attempts to positively integrate sexuality often seem out of kilter. It's like the pendulum swings too far and takes a rather crass turn. Married Christians are encouraged to have wild, rampant sex.

Conferences help women be sexy for their men, with workshops on makeup, lingerie, how to develop vaginal muscles and so on. Husbands speak proudly and publicly about their "smoking hot" wives. I'm often left feeling both squeamish and offended!

> A source of the intensest pleasure earthlings can experience, sex has also been a source of vexatious trouble for the human family since the beginning of history.
>
> **Vernon Grounds**

Christians are not the only ones who can't seem to get a balance or put sexuality into perspective. It has confounded and confused people from the beginning of time, enough so that the early church fathers gave considerable attention to it—for better or worse.

SEX IS HISTORY

Origen was one of the most important philosopher-theologians of the early church. And yet he is perhaps remembered more famously for castrating himself. Fearing that his sexuality would hinder his spirituality, he took Matthew 19:12 literally ("and there are *also* eunuchs who made themselves eunuchs for the sake of the kingdom of heaven" [NASB]) and cut off his genitals. He did later renounce this rather literal translation of the text—a bit late perhaps for his offending organs![1]

As you might imagine, Origen championed celibacy as a virtue. Later church leaders, such as Ambrose in the fourth century, affirmed his views on celibacy, asserting that virginity was a unique and purer form of spirituality. Ambrose encouraged married priests (who were not yet prohibited from marriage) to stop all sexual contact with their wives.

Jerome took this a step further, asserting that because of the sinful associations of sex, Mary the mother of Jesus could not have had a sex life—before, during *and after* giving birth to Jesus. He was also known to say that the only good thing about marriage was that "it produces virgins." (He also suggested that if life is going too well for you, you should "take a wife." Quite the feminist!)[2]

Augustine not only struggled with his own sex life until midlife, he had a seriously conflicted understanding of sex and pleasure. First, he maintained that original sin was passed on through the act of sex. He then went on to say that marital sex itself was sinless if only done for the purpose of procreation. The pleasure one felt in the act of sex was the sinful element and therefore to be suppressed and avoided. It is this distinctive understanding of *concupiscence* (fleshly appetites) that was conferred onto the later church.

It's easy to roll our eyes at what is evidently weird theology (along with some very bizarre behavior). But like us, these folk were trying to work out how sexuality fitted (or not) within their spirituality. These early church fathers were steeped in a Greek understanding of life and reality, rather than a Hebraic one. Hellenistic thinking was innately dualistic, particularly as it related to the body. Anything physical (in this case the body) was of a lower nature, contrary to the spirit and therefore not to be indulged.[3] Anything of the mind was spiritual and to be pursued. Therefore denying the body of any pleasure was taking the higher, more enlightened path.

In direct contrast, Hebraic thought affirmed both mind and matter as good and part of the created order. While one could "sin" with the body (and in sexuality), the body itself (along with sexuality) was to be affirmed as part of God's good creation.

Reformers such as Calvin and Luther took steps in the right direction by rejecting celibacy as more "spiritual" and affirming marriage and marital sex as gifts from God. But dualistic views of body and sexuality have remained overwhelmingly predominant throughout Western church history. What we understand today as Puritanism, with its roots in Reformed understanding, has never been able to get over its deep suspicion of sex, pleasure and the body. It was this stream of Puritanism that I encountered early on in my newfound Christian life and which registered as such a profound disconnect.

Nevertheless, at least one can affirm the profound commitment of the early church to sexual purity. I mean, who today is going to emulate the likes of an Origen? That's a commitment even if it is somewhat ignorant. And given the prevailing cultural influences of broader society, we can perhaps also appreciate how they came to their weird conclusions about sex.

CRAMPED SEXUALITY

When I first came to faith, I shared a bed with my best friend, Mark. This wasn't about sex; both of us had been living and identifying as gay people. We were being practical; the communal house we all lived in had way more people than bedrooms. We had grown up together, and we were more like siblings than friends, so we didn't think twice about our bed situation.

Over time, however, we did begin to wonder, and we eventually asked our pastor, Pat, what he thought. He knew our story, so he wasn't quick to give a yes or no but wisely pointed us to broader Christian principles, encouraging us to ask God. We did, and concluded that it was probably best for us not to share the same bed, so we sold our queen-size waterbed (I know!) and purchased bunk beds instead. We stayed together in that same room until we went off to seminary.

That's when things got even more interesting. On the application form there was a space to write down your preferred roommate. Without hesitation Mark and I put down each other's names. You might deem this as naive, but we really didn't think for a minute it would be a problem. We were best friends, had spent much of our lives together and were already sharing a room. But then we were called in to meet with the dean of students. This was one tough lady. She explained in no uncertain terms that sharing rooms was totally forbidden. It was offensive even to ask. Not only could we not share rooms, but we wouldn't even be allowed into each other's rooms!

A friend tells me that the seminary where she works still operates

under the same puritan rules. Now I can appreciate *some* of the rea-
soning behind this, but I must confess to being struck when she told
me that even male and female siblings aren't allowed to share the
same house. Perhaps even more strangely, singles are not allowed to
share accommodation with married couples. Why? Because it just
doesn't look right—and one never knows what might happen!

Really? Is this what "greater is he that is within you" looks like in
practice? Whatever happened to finding the image of God in the
other? What about nurturing meaningful friendships? Does salvation in Christ really amount to never having any informal connection with members of the opposite sex?

All this highlights once again our somewhat weird relationship to
sexuality. One would have to ask whether we have indeed succumbed
to a view of human nature which, as author Lisa Gee puts it, "at its
most dumbed-down figures us semi-repressed sex drives on legs."[4]

UPTIGHT AND LOCKED DOWN

I know that in most cases these types of rules are coming from a
sincere place, and in certain settings may be appropriate. But let's
not be naive as to what messages they are communicating. First and
fundamentally they effectively reduce the totality of human sexuality to brute sex. Second, they suggest that all men and women are
always sexually attracted to each other. Third, they assume that
people can't help themselves; they simply have to indulge temptation at every possible opportunity!

This form of prohibitive repression of sexual expression actually
runs the risk of cultivating what can be called the forbidden fruit
syndrome—the temptation to possess what we know we can't have
(Romans 7). Rules without a reasoned approach might work for
adolescents, but they are unlikely to work for adults. (Actually, they
don't really work for adolescents either.) And ironically, they take
no account of same-sex attraction. I'm reminded of the time I
booked a Christian camping site for our annual retreat. The retreat

manager warned me that there was to be absolutely no mixing of
the sexes. We were happy to comply, but were secretly smiling. His
rules weren't likely to help much in our
case; about a third of our community were
same-sex attracted! This mindset also
feeds into what has been dubbed the "romantic myth," which elevates marriage or
genital connection as superior to all other
forms of relationship. Hardly helpful for
those who will not marry or who are cur-
rently single, which happens to be 50 percent of the American
population over the age of eighteen.[5]

> Uptight Christians forget
> the fundamental fact
> that God *created* sex.
>
> **Philip Yancey**

Simply imposing distance between men and women doesn't help
them to learn to navigate relationships meaningfully—an activity
we actually have to do every day of our lives. Artificial boundaries
don't exist in the real world, so how can we be authentic disciples,
living examples of healthy humanity, while not being able to relate
meaningfully to at least half of any given population? Are we really
to be that fearful about the other? Is sexual temptation just too hard
to resist? Is all this uptightness really what God intended? Whatever
happened to the call to live in free obedience to God? Augustine
calls free will "the dreaded gift"—dreaded because it gets us into so
much trouble, but a gift because it is also the mechanism by which
we can get out of trouble. We need to learn to use it properly, which
means we need to find ourselves in situations that require it. The
cramped sexuality of puritanism might come from the right motivation of "staying pure," but adults need to be able to make *meaningful decisions for themselves,* not just acquiesce to rules imposed
from the outside.

TOO FREUDIAN?

Dan Brennan breathes a breath of fresh air into cross-gender relationships in his book *Sacred Unions, Sacred Passions.* His is one of

the few books I have read that deals both realistically and appropriately with Christian relationships. He says we must not capitulate to Freudian ideas about sexuality, which "genitalize" all cross-sex relationships, and if taken to their logical conclusion would just about eliminate friendship altogether. To do this we risk losing the gift of shared intimacy that can be found in relationships, even cross-gender ones.[6]

Brennan suggests that two dominant narratives told in Christian communities have held captive our understanding of friendship. The first is the "marital/romantic story," and the second is the "danger story."

> Both stories, of course, involve an introduction, a plot, and a climax towards the same thing: *sex*. Freud, no doubt, would heartily endorse these two stories. But are we to settle for only Freudian sexual formation in our faith communities? As Protestants, we have to ask ourselves, why do we reduce deep, male-female intimacy in our communities to the great Freudian "sex charade"? If the church is going to present an alternative eschatological community of brothers and sisters bonded together as *one* in Christ, formation and friendship must suggest that Christian sexuality has multiple paths for men and women.[7]

Where are the redemptive stories in evangelical culture—stories of healthy nonromantic cross-sex friendships? Brennan proposes the brother-sister metaphor found in Scripture (Mark 3:35) as a third way for men and women to connect in nonsexual intimacy. This vision is a powerful alternative to the prevailing fearful approach to cross-sex friendships.[8]

MODEST MODESTY?

What about modesty? Aren't boundaries just a reflection of our good desire to uphold a sense of this oft-forgotten virtue, one which author Wendy Shalit calls our "lost friend"?[9] No doubt some boundaries naturally arise from a good, wholesome modesty, a sense of knowing what is or isn't appropriate. But I'm not convinced all boundaries arise from this same intent.

Writer Havelock Ellis once said that as it pertains to sexuality, modesty could be at times defined as an "almost instinctive fear."[10] This is precisely where and why we need to be careful. Christians are not to be fear-driven people. Modesty and prudishness are not the same, regardless of how similar they sometimes look.

My sense is that fear, rather than freedom, has become our prime motivator when it comes to sexuality. This is seen perhaps nowhere clearer than in our attempts to both control and regulate it. The old dictum "we fear what we don't understand, and we judge what we fear" explains a lot. And it's not hard to see how and where this works out in our own lives and within broader society. Let's see how this can play itself out:

- We fear sexuality because it seems too hot to handle. We don't understand it or know how to navigate the passion involved. We find it hard to make the connections between our sexuality and our spirituality, which seem to be going in opposite directions.

- As a result sexuality is viewed as a dangerous paganizing force in our souls and in society. Unredeemed and unredeemable, it takes us far from God and godliness.

- Discipleship is therefore viewed as asexual at best, antisexual at worst, requiring the suppression of all the dangerous energy it produces.

- No one really talks about it. Our saints, our heroes, seem to exemplify a disembodied sexlessness, which only confirms our fears.

- The resulting lack of understanding and integration of sexuality breeds fear.

- Fear (particularly in the context of a religious institution, e.g., the church) takes on a life of its own. This causes systematic regulating of the feared thing (in this case sexuality) in order to control the "unknown" monster.

- When "rules" are broken (which they inevitably are) the violator is judged, sometimes publicly, even ejected.
- Rules are then reinforced. Fear levels become elevated. Now even "outsiders" need to conform to sexual purity codes in order to gain entry.

Theologian Ted Peters calls fear "a moral issue in so far as it shapes the kind of people we become."[11] When we are fearful as disciples or as a church, "we begin thinking primarily about what we want to prevent and avoid rather than what we want to encourage and develop."[12] In other words we end up focusing on the wrong things!

FEAR-BASED COUNSEL

I had just finished leading a workshop on sexuality and was packing up my things when I noticed a young man nervously hovering around. I knew he needed to talk so I waited for the room to clear and gently approached him. His color and the look on his face revealed his embarrassment. As soon as we found a private place to talk he burst into tears and in between his sobs poured out his story. He longed to be married and have a family, but for some reason was convinced he'd ruined his chances.

I was trying to imagine what he could possibly have done to warrant such self-recrimination when he stutteringly confessed to me that he'd been masturbating. Nodding gently, I tried to pry out from him something more sinister, but there was nothing more. Yet this kid was clearly devastated. He went on to explain to me that his pastor had warned him that each time he masturbated another mark went against his possibility of having a happy marriage. He was convinced he'd used up all his chances.

It takes a lot for me to go against a pastor's advice, especially someone I know, but on this day I did. I first had to pray for him to be released from the sense of deep shame he was carrying. Then I explained to him that God created him *and* his sexuality, that meant first and foremost it was a good thing. The fact that he felt sexual urges meant that he was at least functional! Isn't this where our sexual counsel should begin? It's one thing to suppress sexuality; it's another to order it appropriately. A proper sexual ethic doesn't deny the fact that we are sexual beings; it develops a framework for the good expression of our good sexuality.

Our young people don't need fear-based counsel that compounds the shame they already feel. This only keeps their sexuality in the dark. Suppressing sexuality doesn't help anyone; transformation starts with acceptance and integration. In marrying sexuality to fear, shame and guilt we have not only tainted God's gracious gift but we have imprisoned his people. All humans are profoundly sexual as well as deeply spiritual creatures—*at the same time*. Failing to integrate the two can cause us to live a fragmented life that operates at two contradictory levels: a disembodied spirituality that floats two inches above the earth, *and* a suppressed bodily sexuality that seeks to find expression in illicit relationships or in sleazy porn.

SEX AND TOTEM POLES

Part of the problem is that we have created a hierarchy of sin, with sexual sins at the top. Think of the way we disciple young believers as a case in point. What is one of the first things we try to get "cleaned up" when someone decides to follow Jesus? Their sex life. We don't hassle them about how they spend their money, their relationship to the poor, their gossiping or their temper. No, we ask them about what they are doing with their genitals—as if this is the principal thing God is concerned about.

I encountered this type of "totem poling" when I posted on Facebook that I was thinking of watching *The Tudors*, a BBC series on King Henry VIII, his wives and the key events around the Reformation.

Within minutes Christians were cautioning me about the sex scenes (that they had evidently watched!). After watching it for two seasons I concluded that the sex scenes were minimal in comparison to other things. Each episode was full to the brim with malicious gossip, treachery, manipulation, violence and murder—oft times at the hands of so-called Christians and church leaders! I didn't receive one warning about these things. John Piper's recent caution of watching the show exemplifies this. His "Twelve Questions to Ask Before Watching 'Game of Thrones'" are *only* to do with the sex scenes![13]

I'm not sure how we arrived at such inconsistent views on how we rate sin. Perhaps it's because Paul talks about sexual sins as having different consequences. He tells us that *sexual* sins are sins made against the body. They have an internal dimension to them, one that we will carry with us (1 Corinthians 6:18). But Paul is also careful to list sexual sins with a whole host of other sins (see 1 Corinthians 6; 1 Timothy 1:8-11), letting us know that while sins might have different consequences, all sins are *equal* before God.

Greg Boyd, in his book *Repenting of Religion*, highlights this inconsistency:

> If we retained a system of evaluating sin at all, sins such as impatience, unkindness, rudeness, and self-righteousness— all indications that love is absent (1 Cor. 13:4-5)—as well as prevalent "church" sins such as gossip, greed, and apathy would rank higher on our list than sins such as homosexuality or heterosexual promiscuity.[14]

It seems to me that when we look to Jesus and his assessment of sin, it looks very different from the puritan code that prevails in many churches. Where we are tempted to put sexual sin at the top of the pile, Jesus names greed and pride. Money and wealth—*not* sex—are for Jesus what is most likely to compete with God for our loyalty (Matthew 6:24). Where we are likely to simply expel sexual sinners, Jesus seems to be very merciful and gracious with them (John

4:1-26; 8:1-11). As much as Jesus cares about the totality of our lives, I sometimes wonder whether Jesus is concerned more by what we do with our money than what we do with our genitals!

In *Untamed*, the book that Alan and I coauthored, we consider the consequences of the sin of adultery:

> Its ramifications include betrayal, relational breakdown, impact on families and friends, and loss of personal integrity. Recovery from adultery, including learning to trust again and to forgive, is difficult and may take a long time to work through, perhaps even a lifetime. All in all, pretty serious consequences.

But look what happens when we consider the consequences of the sin of greed.

> A study by the World Institute for Development Economics Research at United Nations University reports that the richest 1 percent of adults alone owned 40 percent of global assets in the year 2000, and that the richest 10 percent of adults accounted for 85 percent of the world total. The bottom half of the world adult population owned barely 1 percent of global wealth. Now we may think that one individual being greedy won't have an impact, but we need to face the reality that if every Christian repented of greed and lived much closer to the simpler ways of Jesus, then we alone could probably solve the world's hunger problem![15]

I draw our attention to this comparison *not* to minimize sexual sin but rather to highlight the inconsistency and the false hierarchy of sins within the church. Hear priest and author Richard Rohr:

> *The body seems to be where we carry our sense of shame and inferiority*, and early-stage religion has never gotten much beyond these "pelvic" issues. As Jesus put it, "You ignore the weightier matters of the law—justice, mercy, and good faith . . . and instead you strain out gnats and swallow camels" (Matthew 23:23-24).

We worry about what people are doing in bed much more than making sure everybody has a bed to begin with. . . .

Christianity will regain its moral authority when it starts emphasizing social sin in equal measure with individual (read "body-based") sin and weave them both into a seamless garment of love and truth.[16]

THE DISTORTED LENS

Our fear of sexuality and the corresponding inability to integrate our sexuality into our spirituality causes us to see God and the Scriptures in distorted ways. Texts that talk (negatively) about sexuality and sexual sin become our focus, and we neglect teaching on other sins. As a result, we fail to see the fuller picture of the biblical revelation. The Bible ends up as a book of rules, filled with lists of things we should or should not do, especially when it comes to our sexuality.

Lauren Winner, in her book *Real Sex: The Naked Truth About Chastity*, claims,

We need to ask whether the starting point for a scriptural witness on sex is the isolated quotation of "thou shalt not," or whether a scriptural ethic of sex begins instead with the totality of the Bible, the narrative of God's redeeming love and humanity's attempt to reflect that.[17]

Just like with that young guy who feared he'd ruined his chances of marriage, we all need to embrace our sexuality as God's creation and gift *before* we deal with some of its compulsive sides. We need to see the bigger picture. When we divorce particular verses from the totality of the scriptural witness we are bound to dish out simplistic, theologically limp answers that neither satisfy nor make any real sense of the all-too-real human struggle.

Seeing the Bible as a "rule" book, especially related to sexuality, reflects not only on the God it points to but restricts our capacity to see his good intent in and through creation. For even in the Bible's prohibitions we find that the positive is implied—something good is being affirmed. For instance, if you look at the prohibition of covetousness, what is being affirmed? The call to live with great gratitude and to affirm the dignity of others.

Boundaries *are* certainly important for life and sexuality, and the Bible does give us guidelines, but read through the lens of fear they can become the very prison from which we ourselves need liberating.

THE FORBIDDING GOD?

In his wonderful commentary on Genesis, Walter Brueggemann takes us back to the creation story to highlight the imbalance we have in our understanding of God and his creation:

> Human beings before God are characterized by *vocation, permission, and prohibition*. The primary human task is to find a way to hold the three facets of divine purpose together. Any two of them without the third is surely to pervert life. It is telling and ironic that in the popular understanding of this story, little attention is given the mandate of vocation or the gift of permission. The divine will for vocation and freedom has been lost. The God of the garden is chiefly remembered as the one who prohibits.[18]

When God becomes viewed as merely one who dishes out the rules, it follows that his people become pedantic rule keepers. Ironic, since we know that we can live a morally upright life and still manage to keep God out of the equation—the Pharisees of the New Testament are a clear case in point.

Moral puritanism creates what Greg Boyd calls an idolatrous false religion.[19] When discipleship is narrowed down to jumping through behavioral hoops and ticking the right theological boxes, grace is squeezed out, and we come to see God as just plain impossible to please, like some nasty first-grade teacher or harsh, authoritarian parent. When we reduce Christianity to a negative system where fasting becomes more sacred than feasting, law wins out over grace, and correct theology becomes more important than divine encounter, we in effect become the modern-day Pharisees—whose ministry Jesus was set against.

My hunch is that most of us find it hard to view God as *permissive*—the Creator of all who permits his creation to be what he has made it to be (the Genesis 1–2 refrain, "Let there be . . ."). Even the term *permissive* (in the way most Christians use it) has more negative connotations than positive, especially as it relates to sexuality. If someone is "permissive," they either have "loose" morals or are "liberal" in their theology—both seen as bad.

It is vital in developing a theology of sexuality that we are first recaptured by a vision of the God who permits—the God who first and foremost grants us a resounding yes and rejoices in his creation. As Abraham Heschel says, "God is not only the creator of earth and heaven. He is also the One who created delight and joy. . . . Even lowly merriment originates in holiness. The fire of evil can better be fought with flames of holy ecstasy than through fasting and mortification."[20] The philosopher Martin Buber similarly remarked that of all the works of creation, it is passion which is very good, because without it humans cannot serve God, or truly live.[21]

It's time to turn the page: Readjust the lens with which we view the Scriptures and God. Read the Bible with fresh eyes, eyes that can take in the whole picture, see the full story.

Read afresh, the Bible offers the greatest and most redemptive love story ever told, one filled with all the drama of sexuality in regular life. It's all there: the raw force of human longing, its passion, its pain, even the erotic is captured. The Bible is confronting, embarrassing and even shocking at times—just like real life—because it *is* real life. That's the whole point.

The Bible is written for broken people. God *knows* that we are going to struggle in real life—he is the one who made us in the first place, and our sins are of no great surprise to him. I'm not suggesting a blasé attitude; our pursuit of holiness should be rigorous—for God's sake as well as our own. But I believe it's time to put sexuality (and all its failings) into perspective. We can start doing so by revisiting Jesus, fully divine and, as the Word made flesh, wholly sexual.

Jesus . . . Sex Symbol?

Here's the deal. People are not looking for doctrine. They're looking for a God with skin on, who they can know, speak with, learn from, struggle with, be honest with, get straight answers from, and connect their lives to.

HUGH HALTER

I think most of us find it hard to think of Jesus as having sexual needs. Maybe because Jesus was sinless and we so easily associate sexuality with sin. Whatever the reason, we certainly don't talk much about it. Yet some of the first questions my friends and I asked when we came to faith had to do with Jesus' sexuality.

Given that he was the one we were meant to model our lives after, this seemed perfectly normal. Yet nobody back then was brave enough to talk to us about it—it seemed to be one aspect of his humanity that remained unexplored. But to us a sexless Jesus just didn't seem that human!

The conversations in our motley group ranged from "Was Jesus ever tempted homosexually?" to "What did Jesus do if he became aroused?" and "Did Jesus ever masturbate?" Some might feel uncomfortable with these questions, but they are real questions that people ask, if not out loud then at least in their minds.

One of the problems of not talking about sexuality is that we have inadvertently cultivated a sexless Jesus; we have made God in the image of Origen. Yet, if Jesus is my Lord, my Savior and the model of human holiness that I am to pursue with my life (including my sexuality), then what does his life and work mean for me as a man or a woman, as sexually male or female? This seems to me to be of vital importance for the life of discipleship.

EROS REDEEMED

The first and fundamental thing we need to come to grips with is in fact that Jesus (as a real man) had to have been a *sexual* being or else he was not a human being. Michael Frost underscores this uncertainty we seem to have regarding Jesus' sexuality:

> Jesus really is an enigma to many people and his sexuality is considered to be even more mysterious. When, in the rock opera *Jesus Christ Superstar*, Mary Magdalene sings, "I don't know how to love Him," she expresses the general frustration we all seem to experience regarding our view of Jesus. We're uncertain of how to—or whether to—view him as a sexual being.[1]

Questions about Jesus' sexuality should be normative—they follow the logic of the incarnation. Jesus' sexuality is normative because his humanity is normative. If Jesus lived out his life in a real, physical body with all the longings that go with it—including the sexual—then we certainly need to grapple with it. Theologian Marilyn Sewell's provocative writing about Jesus should give us cause to reflect:

> The Jesus I know is robust—a carpenter, capable of doing heavy work. He is a fleshly man, filled with thankfulness for the beauty of the natural world, and one who enjoys good food and drink. He is a man of great tenderness, not ashamed of his tears. He does not hide his feelings, and goes straight to the heart in a

few words. The Jesus I know enjoys his body and is aware of the wonders of its shape and movement, likes to feel the sun on his limbs, takes pleasure in resting after a long day's journey. He likes the feel of splashing water on his skin when he washes.

And he is a sexual man, one who enjoys being a man, including having a penis, though it is sometimes troublesome for him, demanding attention when he wants to be otherwise occupied. But he accepts that as simply part of what is, like being thirsty or feeling weary or getting angry. Sexuality is part of being human, and it's good. . . .

In his remarkable self-acceptance, Jesus seems to bring new life to whoever comes near. His presence is extraordinarily vital, is fearsome, and calls for a profound response. Jesus is in fact God's invitation to wholeness and self-hood. When we are able to celebrate Jesus in the flesh, we understand that we, too, are called to incarnation, called to embody God's Spirit in our earthly form.[2]

Looking to Jesus as our sexual model forces us to move beyond our fixation with genital sexuality to a much broader view of human sexuality, one that includes nongenital intimacy.

REAL MEN NEED SOME REAL LOVIN'

All of our sexual/relational needs can be summed up in two essential desires or longings, what theologian Marva Dawn calls our *social sexuality* and our *genital sexuality*.[3] Implicit in each of these is what we might experience as the longing to be completed in the other. If indeed Jesus' nature (and body) is just like ours (and God's nature for that matter), then we must assume that there exists a similar compulsion to connect with others. Is not God love? And is not love communal?

Thinking of Jesus as needing to be around people feels a little strange, mostly because we are so versed in the language and experience of *people* needing to be around Jesus. This is evident not only in our own lives but certainly as we engage the Scriptures. It's hard not to be struck, reading the Gospels, with the sheer number of people who pursued him. It was a one-way relationship for sure—the curious, the hungry, the broken, all wanting, *needing* something from him. Yet in the midst of this needy throng of humanity Jesus himself sought out specific people, not only to impart his message, but his life and heart too.

As we take a closer look at Jesus' relationships we begin to see something of the nature of his concrete friendships beyond the clatter and clamor of the crowd. The obvious are those who hung around him throughout much of his journey, those he taught and discipled beyond the masses. The seventy-two he sent out in Luke 10 knew him and his message well enough that in his directions to them he was confident enough to declare, "Whoever listens to you listens to me; whoever rejects you rejects me" (v. 16), suggesting a substantial level of relational trust.

The twelve disciples got to see him up close and personal; they went on the road with him, literally, living, eating, laughing and learning alongside their friend. These are the ones he entrusted his life and ministry to. And of these twelve, the Scriptures seem to indicate that there were three he drew in even closer. Often referred to as Jesus' "inner circle," Peter, James and John were the ones Jesus wanted to be with him for his transfiguration (Matthew 17:1-9), the healing of Jairus's daughter (Mark 5:37-42) and during his time of turmoil in the garden of Gethsemane (Mark 14:32-36). These were

> Jesus has been so zealously worshiped, his deity so vehemently affirmed, his halo so brightly illumined, and his cross so beautifully polished, that in the minds of many he no longer exists as a man. By thus glorifying him we more effectively rid ourselves of him than did those who tried to do so by crudely crucifying him.
>
> Clarence Jordan

pretty powerful and intense times, the times when you only want your close friends around.

Perhaps surprisingly, there were also many women who had intimate friendships with Jesus. Given the culture of the time this is significant. Luke 8:1-3 mentions a number of women, including Mary Magdalene (who we will come back to), Joanna, Susanna and a number of others who were directly involved in supporting Jesus and the twelve disciples. His friendship with Mary and Martha of Bethany appeared to be quite significant. They welcomed Jesus into their home when he was in town, showing him hospitality and extending him friendship, so much so that John, in the retelling of the story of their brother Lazarus, has no qualms declaring, "Jesus *loved* Martha and her sister and Lazarus" (John 11:5). And in John 11:3, in reporting of Lazarus's illness, the two sisters beseech Jesus saying, "Lord, the one *you* love is sick" (John 11:3, italic mine) an emphasis on Jesus' love for him, not the reverse. These are hints at more than a passing or functional connection; they suggest significant and real friendships.

One particularly beautiful thing about Jesus is that his life is testament to the fact that being single doesn't have to equate to being lonely, nor does it exclude enjoying deep levels of intimacy. Jesus, just like us, lived within the relational fabric of community in order to sustain his full humanity.

JOHN THE BELOVED

I love the disciple John; perhaps it's because he speaks so intimately and unashamedly about Jesus. He certainly was the disciple who not only knew his place in Jesus' life and heart, but wanted everyone else to know it! He refers to himself as the "beloved disciple" or the "disciple Jesus loved,"[4] with such ease and confidence—as one author puts it, "Every opportunity that John had to make reference to himself seemed to be an opportunity to celebrate his intimacy with Christ."[5]

John was surely a man who loved his friend and knew his friend loved him. It was he, after all, who got to rest his head on the breast of Jesus at the Last Supper and stayed with him at the cross when the other disciples fled. He was also the first of the Twelve to see the empty tomb, and it was to him that Jesus entrusted the care of his mother (John 19:25-27).

John was, as one author suggests, "one of those rare men 'who appear to be formed of finer clay than their neighbors, and cast in a gentler mold.'"[6] I find it particularly interesting that many of the medieval paintings of John depict him in almost effeminate ways. While just depictions, these images have not been lost on some of my gay friends. Some have wondered about the exact nature of John's love for Jesus—curious as to whether John could have possibly, like them, experienced some form of same-sex attraction. For a lot of my gay friends it makes John (and therefore John's Jesus) more accessible. If Jesus could choose a gay disciple, then he could also choose them.

Whether John (or any of the disciples for that matter) did or did not experience same-sex attraction isn't really the point. I'm reminded of something Mark said to me once when we were younger believers. He told me how he had moved into a new season in his relationship with Jesus; he was now relating to him as heterosexual. I was a bit confused and asked him what he meant, to which he replied, "Well, he has been my perfect lover, the man who would never leave me, never abuse me. He just *loves* me. Now he is also becoming my best friend." In his own way, Mark, a gay man, was navigating his relationship to Jesus, working out what it was to love him.

MARY THE BELOVED

When people do talk about the friendships of Jesus, they focus primarily on his *male* friendships, particularly when they talk about his "inner circle." Yet, as mentioned earlier, there were also a number of women whom Jesus seemed particularly close to—most notably Mary of Magdala. While some have speculated about the nature and unusual depth of his relationship to her (and the Gospel stories suggest it was especially intimate), there is no indication in the

Scriptures that it was ever expressed genitally. But this doesn't mean their relationship was sexually neutral or lacked emotional intensity. Dan Brennan expresses this beautifully,

> Jesus awakened love in her. This was not the distant, calculated kind of love. She opened herself to love this particular man. She was drawn into his passion for people, for life, for God; yet it was not a genital or romantic passion. He was intense. She was intense. She had never met anyone like him. She kept following him while other followers walked away. His messages divided people, yet she saw unmistakable love in him. Then he was crucified. She was compelled to be near him even as others mocked him on the cross. Her love for this particular *man* is not calculating but risky in the hostile atmosphere at the foot of the cross.[7]

Mary, not some genderless being but a real woman with real desires, was drawn into and captivated by this man-God. She experienced the power of his tenderness, the nearness of his physical presence, and was radically healed by his touch. She displays her profound gratitude and love by following him to the cross, staying by his side throughout the whole brutal scene that most others fled from. It's no wonder that it was to her that Jesus revealed himself after his resurrection.

> A woman's heart should be so hidden in God that a man has to seek Him just to find her.
>
> **Maya Angelou[8]**

In Jesus' relationship to both John and Mary we see something unique, something tender. The depth of each would have been both a gift and a source of pain for Jesus. Jim Cotter articulates this well, "Jesus' sexuality was surely alive, however painful it may have been, however restrained in appropriate loving, but also a means of delight and pleasure shared, of creativity and union: to live such a life ourselves is surely not to be far from the Commonwealth of God."[9]

JESUS LOVED WELL

I have often wondered at the sheer power of Jesus' sexuality. He was a fully integrated, completely whole man who would have been deeply attractive to both men and women. And I don't doubt that genital sexual advances were made toward him—we just don't hear about them. Although we do get a glimpse into one very sexually charged environment. At Simon the Pharisee's house (Luke 7:36-50) we encounter a woman—a known prostitute, a woman who lived off her sexuality and body—wetting the feet of Jesus with her perfume and tears, then wiping them with her hair. What a picture! The fact that her hair was loosened (something only done in the intimacy of a bedroom) shows clear erotic overtones—at least on her behalf—and it certainly was not lost on the crowd! Yet Jesus lets her continue.

This is a man who risked great misunderstanding by even allowing this woman physical closeness to himself. Yet he did it. As my friend and church planter Katie Driver says,

> Jesus didn't avoid relationships with women, even with those women who had a history of sexual sin and proclivity. He also didn't avoid being alone with women. His disciples thought it strange, but Jesus wasn't frightened or inhibited from interacting and even befriending women of reputations.[10]

And while it might seem that Jesus walked closer to the line than would most religious men I know, his actions were not reckless but redemptive. In this one act he both redeems sensuality and affirms nongenital contact between men and women. Apparently modern-day puritans would not approve![11]

Jesus had an uncanny ability to be close to both women and men, physically and emotionally, without violating his (or their) sexual integrity. Not only that, when the sexually broken encounter him, his very presence brings with it the offer of freedom. Marva Dawn is on cue when she says, "He [Jesus] kept his *social sexuality* distinct from his *genital sexuality* by relating in powerfully wholesome, up-

building, nongenital ways with persons of both sexes. And frequently his support for 'naughty women' set them free to 'go and sin no more' genitally."[12]

There seemed to be an ease and almost uncomplicated quality about Jesus and the way he related to those close to him. He doesn't seem to have some of the usual hang-ups we in the church have. He wasn't afraid to be intimate with both sexes, nor did he seem to be all that fussy about being alone with women—it seems his boundaries were far less rigorous than ours, yet his sexual integrity remained intact and redemptive. Jesus seems able to create a space between himself and others where real love is able to flourish and where feeling passionate toward another doesn't have to lead to having sex.

Where the church has demarcated clear boundaries between "friends" and "lovers," permitting passion and intensity only in the latter, Jesus blurs the lines, suggesting it is possible to love intensely outside of a marriage relationship. This has to be good news for all of us, especially single folk who feel that such intimacy is unavailable to them, and that their singleness shouts of some form of incompleteness in themselves or the lack of God's blessing in their lives.

At the very least, Jesus as a single person calls us to challenge our culture's capitulation to Freudian understandings of sexuality. And his own single sexuality forces us to call into question the negative and suspicious lens with which we have come to view celibacy and singleness in our time.

JESUS WAS CELIBATE

Thanks to a global sex scandal in the Catholic priesthood, celibacy has been profoundly discredited in our time. But celibacy in the church is a matter that extends far beyond the priesthood. We are now in a context where there are likely to be significantly more single people than marrieds in the church.[13] At the same time, social sexual mores are loosening such that the church increasingly stands alone in expecting people to limit genital sex to marital relationships. What does

Jesus' celibacy have to say to our obsessions with sexual expression?

As someone who has been married for twenty-five years, it's hard for me to speak about celibacy or the single life. But I will say that I am thankful that Jesus was a single man. Not just because he avoided putting a wife and possible children through the trauma of the cross, but because in him we find the redemption of celibacy, and therefore of singleness. And as many of my dear friends (both gay and straight) are walking the celibate path, this gives them a deeper insight and appreciation of what Jesus experienced.

Let's face it, singles in the church today get the raw end of the deal. Not only do they have to navigate isolation and loneliness, but they have to do it in a context that by and large idolizes marriage and family, and therefore focuses much of its resources and attention in that direction. And into this journey steps Jesus, a single man who not only redeems singleness but also has the gumption to redefine family. Jesus breaks the fixation with mere biological bonds and creates a new family where *all* can belong by virtue of their relationship to God through him. There can be no such thing as a *single* person in God's expansive family.

WHAT? JESUS REALLY IS MY BOYFRIEND?

Jean Vanier, author and founder of the worldwide L'Arche communities (and himself a celibate man), talks about the intimacy with God that can develop through celibacy: "Celibacy remains a mystery . . . it has been shown as a special way of uniting oneself with God and preparing oneself to receive a new and more intimate union with him."[14] Valerie certainly had this. Valerie was my spiritual director and my hero. At first I found it odd that she used to wear a wedding ring symbolizing her marriage to Jesus, but then I got it. Her marriage to Jesus was what made the difference between her and me. This woman *knew* God. And her impact in my life was simply profound. I met with her regularly for over six years, and for most of that time I would sit at her feet. She found that a bit weird, but I insisted.

I needed to sit at someone's feet. I needed to learn. And I needed to soak up the Jesus in her. I was drawn to this woman like a magnet. I had never met anyone quite like her; my attraction certainly wasn't genitally motivated, but it was *sexual*. I wanted more of her.

Maybe Valerie was someone who experienced the genuine *gift* of celibacy. She was someone who by her very life gave us a tiny glimpse into what the magic and mystery of the ultimate union with Christ will look like. Vanier again: "Celibacy, for the sake of the Kingdom, answering the call of Jesus, has always been lived in the Church by those who were able to welcome it and to choose it."[15]

Yet the vast majority who walk the celibacy path do so not by choice or gift, but by circumstance. This means celibacy can be a difficult thing to bear, an issue of sacrificial discipleship. It flows out of a relationship and commitment to follow Jesus—no matter what. It does involve loss, but as Philip Yancey observes, "A life of resisting temptation and purity [also] involves . . . the very gain promised by Jesus in the Beatitudes."[16] And it is this extraordinary reward that can sometimes make spiritual giants out of celibate Christians.

Perhaps this is what Paul is getting at in his letter to the Corinthians:

> I would like you to be free from concern. An unmarried man is concerned about the Lord's affairs—how he can please the Lord. But a married man is concerned about the affairs of this world—how he can please his wife—and his interests are divided. An unmarried woman or virgin is concerned about the Lord's affairs: Her aim is to be devoted to the Lord in both body and spirit. But a married woman is concerned about the affairs of this world—how she can please her husband. I am saying this for your own good, not to restrict you, but that you may live in a right way in undivided devotion to the Lord. (1 Corinthians 7:32-35)

Many of my other spiritual heroes have navigated the peculiar path of celibacy. Mother Teresa, Jean Vanier, Henri Nouwen, Jim Cotter and Richard Rohr all took vows of celibacy. Others remained celibate till their later years: C. S. Lewis only married at age fifty-nine. Still others remained celibate their whole lives without taking formal religious orders that required it. John Stott, for example, saw his singleness as a gift and said that God was faithful in supporting those he calls to it.[17] These few and many others who we learn deep and rich truths from are all celibate, formally or informally, for a time or for life. All have that thing, that something special, that little unique insight into God.

And it is exactly this type of mystery that brings us back once again to the connection that exists between sexuality and spirituality. For here we see the marrying of the longings for God and others.

JESUS CONNECTS THE DOTS

In Jesus we find the perfect marrying of sexuality and spirituality. He is the living embodiment of what a completely integrated spirituality and sexuality look like. Not only does he provide a model for us in

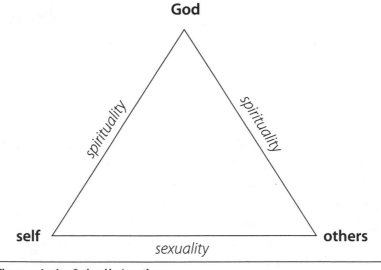

Figure 3.1. Loving God and loving others.

himself, but he points to the way for us to attain it. This is captured nowhere more succinctly than in the proclamation and the living out of the two greatest commandments: loving God and loving others (see fig. 3.1).

The first and greatest commandment is to love God with all our heart, soul, mind and strength. Is this not spirituality—*knowing God and being known by him, loving God and being loved by him*? This is represented as our vertical longing.

The second commandment is to love our neighbor as ourselves. Is this not (to a large degree) our sexuality—*knowing others and being known by them, loving others and being loved by them*? This is represented as our horizontal longing.

It should be clear by now that I'm not saying Jesus is commanding us to "love" God and have "sex" with others. Rather, he is calling us to be in "right" loving relationship with God and with people. Isn't this after all what God is all about—righteous and holy love? For some, genital sexuality is part of that right loving, but for others holiness toward God is going to mean walking the path of celibacy as Jesus did, developing right, good and life-giving relationships.

To love God is to walk in his ways. And the *Shema*—that great commandment of the Old Testament commended by Jesus—gives us the needed focus (love God) and therefore the needed perspective on loving others.

It's important to remember that not only are these commandments the summation of all the Law and Prophets, they are the *highest* of all the commandments. Why? Because they provide the essential guideline for how we best function as humans. God made us both spiritual and sexual, and Jesus points us to them saying, "Do them and you will live," knowing that our obedience to them will bring us life—for this is exactly what we were created for!

Dan Brennan, in his book *Sacred Unions Sacred Passions*, poses a very important question to a church whose view of sexuality is captured by fear:

What would our marriages, our friendships, our churches, and our communities look like if men and women were not afraid of connecting with each other in deep ways? What if men and women could really know each other without sex getting in the way? What if we did not have to be so afraid of our own and others' bodies that we cannot trust ourselves with them?[18]

I guess we would look a whole lot more like Jesus! In Jesus, the fully integrated human, the embodiment of spirituality and sexuality, we find *our* model: a man whose life was characterized by *right* loving, who navigated well both genital and social aspects of his sexuality. If Jesus' model and his rule of life (living out the two greatest commandments) became our model, then no matter who we are (gay, straight, transgender, etc.) or where we find ourselves (relationally speaking) we would not only look a whole lot more like Jesus, but we would become great lovers!

Part Two

BITS, BOBS AND
TRICKY BUSINESS

The Eight
Fundamentals of Sex

*People are looking not for a no-holds barred sexuality
but for a sexuality to be defined more broadly than the
erotic. The flagrant sexuality of MTV and sitcoms gives
us a reduction of the expansive life-affirming motivation
that our sexuality is. But people are longing for a broadening of what it means to be a sexual person.*

LILIAN CALLES BARGER

My mother's way of educating me about all things sexual was to
hand me a copy of the book *Every Woman*, tell me to read it and
then on her way out of my room mumble something like, "Anyway,
you probably know more about sex than me."

I was thirteen. And I didn't. Well, I'd never had sex, if that's what
she'd meant. But I was about to embark on a rapid learning curve—
I had just started going out with an older guy, and he was way more
eager than my mother to teach me.

All of us *will* learn one way or another about sex and sexuality—
the good, the bad and the ugly—for it has all those sides. Poets and
artists put words, images and voice to the deep emotions we feel.
Anthropologists, psychologists and the like help us to understand

ourselves in relation to the *other*—revealing our motivations and exposing our hidden pathos. Biologists teach us all about our bits and bobs and how they all work together. And of course the Scriptures provide the bigger picture, giving us the *why* of sexuality and helping provide a framework for *how* we best function as sexual beings.

Each of these fields adds greater insight to help plunder the mystery and mechanics of our sexuality. But no matter how much we learn, it's never complete. It involves continual learning. It has to, because it's about life and love and relationships—and who knows all there is to know about such things? And sexuality will continue to surprise, confuse and even mislead us—again and again. But that's half the fun—isn't it?

This chapter is about eight simple fundamentals that I've learned about sexuality along the way, things I'm sure my mother would have taught me had she known.

1. SEXUALITY: TWO ESSENTIAL IMPULSES

I was first introduced to the terms *genital sexuality* and *social sexuality* in Marva Dawn's wonderful book *Sexual Character*.[1] She uses them to help distinguish the two types of relational drives humans experience, suggesting that *every* relationship we have (to varying degrees) is socially motivated, and only some are genitally motivated.[2] Let me expand each of them as I have developed them for my purposes.

Social sexuality constitutes all the relationships we have: family, friends, work colleagues and so on—all those that make up our basic social network and friendship circles. Each relationship we have provides different levels of intimacy with different levels of intensity. We each have a range of needs that are met through a variety of people. Every relationship we have therefore fits somewhere into the category of *social* sexuality.

Genital sexuality has to do with our genital sexual connection and longing. This can range from a purely physical act (if there is such a thing) to experiencing all the stuff of romance, fluttering of the heart, arousal and so forth. On some level this involves a degree of *nakedness*—certainly physically, but also emotionally and even spiritually. And while expressions of genital sexuality can be divorced from the engagement with another person (e.g., masturbation, self-stimulation, etc.), in its ideal expression sexuality is about relational engagement with another.

Dawn gives a personal example of how the two aspects of sexuality play themselves out:

> Our social sexuality is composed of all aspects of our being that are distinct from specific feelings, attitudes, or behaviors related or leading to genital union. When I speak with you I do not do so as a neuter. I relate to you as a woman, with my particular body and spirit and mind, with my whole self, which has discovered its identity within the framework of my being female. How I relate to everyone else in the world in every kind of human interaction depends upon the way in which my social sexuality has been formed. I write, I teach, buy groceries, or talk with someone on an airplane out of my social sexuality. Also in my own unique personality, in social situations I express a woman's affection in many ways—hugs, touches, kisses, words—but these are carefully chosen to be fully loving and honorable, thoroughly reserving all expressions of genital sexuality for one and only one person, my husband.[3]

Dawn then traces both of these essential longings back to the creation narratives in Genesis. Here we see the scriptural presentation of God's design for *genital* sexuality: "In Genesis 2:24 the man is commanded to leave his father and mother and cleave to his wife. . . . The result is a new family unit and unity, especially marked by the covenantal sign of genital union." And God's design for *social* sexuality: "Quite distinctly, Genesis 1:26-27 proclaims liturgically the creation of human beings as the culmination of God's sovereign, harmonious ordering of the world. Human beings are especially created to image God, and a significant part of that imaging is fellowship [*social* sexuality]. In our relationships with each other, we model the community of the Trinity."[4]

The Genesis texts help us to understand our sexuality in two fundamental ways: First, as part of God's good created order, which means that God created us sexual, and being sexual is good! That means we can freely let go of all those negative attitudes we carry around about sex.[5] And second, in some way being sexual is connected to the way we image our Creator—now that's something to think about!

Now make no mistake, it's easy to put *social* and *genital* sexuality into two neat categories when you are writing about them, but we all know that the truth of the matter is that they are not always so neatly divided. For example, many of us confuse them all the time, or simply replace one with the other. This can happen when we substitute (or mistake) intimacy with sex. In other words we can think that by simply engaging in some *genital* sexual act, our *social* sexual needs (our need for intimacy) will somehow be filled. And while sex might deliver many things, genuine love is not always one of them! In fact, as Hollywood so powerfully demonstrates, unconditioned sex can invoke some of the worst aspects of our nature, including will to power, submission, cruelty, jealousy and possessiveness, among others. Few other things can awaken the dark elements residing in every human heart as well as lust.

A potent insight into the nature of lust and love came from a client of mine; let's call him Justin. Justin, in his own words, was "controlled by sex" and regularly visited gay beats,[6] sometimes several times a day. On one such visit a man came into the bathroom that he found attractive. In order to signal his offer for sex, Justin held his hand out toward him. The man took his hand, held it and looked straight into Justin's eyes. Justin said when their eyes connected it was like time stood still. The man's eyes were filled with such gentleness and warmth it was hard to break the stare. When he finally broke his gaze, the man let go of Justin's hand, turned and silently walked away. Justin said at this point he began to shake uncontrollably. In looking into that man's eyes he had seen something resembling real love. It was a defining moment of revelation for him, because he realized that it wasn't really raw sex he desired, he needed to be loved and held by a man. I remember Justin wondering whether God sent an angel to visit him that day in the public restroom.

"Falling in love" type feelings are another source of confusion for many people. We often equate intensity of feeling with genital longing, thinking that if I feel especially strongly toward someone it means I must want to, or I should, have sex with him or her. But having intense emotional attraction doesn't have to

> Beneath the search for genital sexuality is a longing to be loved. One seeks it where one can.
>
> Jean Vanier

equate to genital longing. For example, I could say that I have "fallen in love" with more people than I've wanted to have sex with. Valerie, my long-term spiritual director, falls into that category. The feelings I felt for her had a level of intensity that caught me off-guard. I *knew* my attraction wasn't erotic (or genital) in nature, but I was definitely *attracted* to her. My best friend at school was another case in point. My mother was convinced we were lesbians because our relationship was so intense and all-consuming. And while I had at that point never felt so close to another person, I did not once feel erotically drawn to her, or her to me for that matter. Just a few years later I did experience erotic desires for a woman, but I did not have near the intensity or emotional depth of feeling I had with my other friend.

The intensity you feel when you "fall in love" in ways just described is very similar to romantic love, just without the erotic component. And just like its romantic cousin, this type of love seems to enhance *everything*; it's like somehow the world becomes a much brighter place. You hear birds singing, the sun shining, flowers blooming, all in a way you didn't before the other person came along. You feel truly and transcendently more *connected*. And isn't this exactly what love is meant to do? But just like romantic love, this love also settles down. Within the give and take of relationship we begin to see each other a little more clearly, our need becomes less intense, and security begins to settle in. This is where our friendship grows and matures in deeper ways. Without giving relationships real time, it's hard for love to grow and develop—real love is only cultivated over the long haul.

Over the years a number of young Christian women have come to me questioning such feelings. Because of the intensity they shared for one another, they have wondered whether they might actually be gay. And while some were same-sex attracted, most were simply experiencing feelings that seemed like they belonged in a fully *sexual* relationship. Mistaking these feelings is not necessarily uncommon among women, and the situation is made more complex by the apparent fluidity of women's sexuality and the social and physical ease we have with each other compared to men. The gap between "gay" and "straight" is not often as clear for women as it is for men. Perhaps this accounts for the rise in women who identify as bisexual.[7]

Sexuality can certainly be confusing. The feelings we experience are sometimes very hard to navigate, which is why we need to take the time to understand ourselves, the particular desires and needs that draw us, the particular people we are drawn to. Even with a moderate level of self-insight, we can learn to steer our attractions toward healthy, life-giving relationships.

2. SEXUALITY IS TRANSGENITAL

If it's not obvious by now, one of the fundamental things we need to appreciate about sexuality is that it doesn't just reside in our groin regions. Sexuality is written through every aspect of who we are. We

because just *being* a girl caused her pain. The result of this was that Sam cultivated a pretty strong masculine identity—looking and behaving like a boy provided Sam with a much-needed refuge.

We met Sam when she was in her late teens, and by that time she had so nurtured this masculine look that most people who met her thought she was a guy. Having a nondescript gender name didn't help matters. Sam used to pretend it didn't matter, but I could see the hurt look in her eyes every time it happened. She might have looked and acted like a guy on the outside, but she longed to be loved and accepted as a woman on the inside.

It's easy to see in Sam's story the interconnectedness of sexuality. Her experience of genital sexual abuse affected her growing sense of gender identity, causing her to disconnect from her femininity, and this in turn affected all her social and genital relationships. She even became confused about who she should date, not because she was naturally attracted to other women but because she looked and carried herself like a guy.

3. SEXUALITY IS EMBODIED

"Trixie Bell" was a finely constructed alter ego of one of the prostitutes I came to know. Complete with red wig and false eyelashes, Trixie Bell worked in a parlor and kept her "work" and alter ego as far away as she could from who she was in her regular life. This was not only important for the stability of her emotions but also for the two young kids she was raising. The problem with alter egos is they only work for a while.

Many of the prostitutes I knew constructed some sort of alter ego, even those who worked on the street. While not as concerned with wigs and other paraphernalia, they still sought to separate themselves from the work they did. One of the familiar comments I would hear was, "It's not *me* having sex, it's just my body." Many had come to view their bodies as simply "tools of their trade," thinking that they could shut themselves off (psychologically and emotionally speaking) from what their bodies were doing.

And while it might seem to work in the short term, it is simply impossible to completely divorce ourselves (our personhood, our souls) from what we do with our bodies.[11] We are not, as Stanley Grenz says, "primarily and essentially souls and secondarily and consequently bodies." Rather, from original creation to the new creation we are embodied beings. Our personhood and sexuality are tied together with the fact that we are "flesh and blood."[12]

This is one of the things being addressed in 1 Corinthians 6:15-17.[13] Paul is at pains to make the point that what we do with our bodies matters, and that they belong to the Lord. And if one joins him- or herself to a prostitute, they become "one flesh." Paul's point here is not to moralize about prostitution but rather to highlight the impact of sexuality on our embodied selves. What happens to our bodies happens to us. As my friend Rowland says, "Because it involves the splitting up of a person, prostitution is a foretaste of hell, not of heaven. For in heaven all things will be united in Christ, including all our parts: body, mind, spirits, emotions, wills."[14]

It's taken me years to get more in touch with my body, to begin to love it and get to know it, learn to *feel* it (and I'm not just talking about shape and size here). When I am able to integrate my spirituality *with* my body, including all its desires and pleasures, I do feel more fully alive, more whole, more integrated. When I fail to do this by neglecting its health and well-being, it becomes something I respond to in purely functional ways. And this is to the detriment of both my sexuality as well as my spirituality, for they are intrinsically tied in together.

I love what author Christopher West says of our bodies: "The body, in fact, and it alone . . . is capable of making visible what is invisible: the spiritual and divine. It was created to transfer into the visible reality of the world, the mystery hidden since time immemorial in God, and thus to be a sign of it."[15] Think about that for a minute. Our bodies can be the very place where something of the mystery of God is revealed. And while I've yet to appreciate the full implications of what West is saying, I know it's a great challenge, particularly in the church where dualistic understandings of the body seem to prevail.

This means we must embrace our bodies as an essential part of who we are. We can't disconnect ourselves from what we do with them. Neither can we, like Origen, reject certain parts of them, even in attempts to be more spiritual. Our souls are revealed in and through our bodies—they "make visible" the invisible reality of our spirits, and because we are made in God's image, our bodies also make visible something of God's invisible mystery.[16]

4. SEXUALITY CELEBRATES DIFFERENCE

In case you hadn't noticed, men and women navigate and express sexuality somewhat differently. For example, if we could say that *social sexuality* exists more in the realm of emotion and heart, and *genital sexuality* more in the realm of physicality, body and contact, then it's not too hard to see what I'm talking about. Men (generally) are more genitally motivated, women (generally) are more socially motivated. And while I'm loathe to make such broad generalizations, God did indeed make two *different* sexes, implication being that we would express ourselves, particularly in that relational side of us (our sexuality), differently. And research seems to back this up.

Studies in genital expressions of sexuality overwhelmingly conclude that it is more the domain of the male. In summarizing these studies, the Balswicks conclude,

> Men's attitudes and behaviors are characterized as more non-relational sexuality and female sexuality as relational. For instance men are found to masturbate more than women, hold more sexually permissive attitudes, regard casual intercourse positively, be more sexually promiscuous.[17]

It seems that men do think about sex and seek it out more than most women.[18] This tendency is also confirmed in gay relationships.

A major study conducted by Philip Blumstein and Pepper Swartz concluded that "gay men had much higher frequencies of sex than lesbians at all stages of relationships."[19] It does tend to make theological and psychological sense to me that if God created the sexes with different sexual needs (so to speak) and with an innate complementarity in nature, then in a same-sex relationship the sexual biases of each partner would be exaggerated.

And while it should not surprise us, women really *are* more complicated than men. And this is also seen in the way they express sexuality. Not only is a woman's sexuality more fluid, but women experience orgasms differently, take a less direct route in getting there, are more choosey about their partners, and are more likely to be influenced by social and cultural factors.[20] This research seems to confirm that women are more *socially* sexually driven than men.

An interesting way to see our sexual differences play out is to look at the types of magazines we read. Magazines as a medium are indicators of where people's interests lie. For instance, the highest selling men's magazines fall into the category of "soft porn"— magazines like *Playboy* (genital sexual interest). For women it's *Women's Day*, *Who Weekly* and the like (social sexual interest). It seems men have a penchant for looking at people's private parts, women for looking into people's private lives.

Maybe another way of saying it would be that men tend toward objectifying sexuality, focusing on external stimuli, genital connection, fetishizing of objects, physical power and so on. Women on the other hand tend toward the more subjective aspects inherent in sexuality (e.g., the emotional, relationship, romance, psychological power, etc.). And needless to say while these differences are highlighted in research, there will always be some who don't fit neatly into these categories.

It's important to note here that whether gay or straight, male or female, our differences (or similarities) are not simply a matter of nature but nurture. One obvious example is the fact that men (culturally speaking) are encouraged to be more sexually assertive than women. It is simply more socially acceptable.

When viewed holistically, though, sexuality ought to maintain a balance between the two. Men ought to experience subjective sexuality while the women engage more of the objective aspects of it.

5. SEXUALITY IS FRACTURED

It's important for us to remember that all our experience of sexual life has been affected by the fall. In other words, the ramifications of sin are felt on every level of our sexuality—in our bodies, in our distortions of gender (and identity), and in the way we relate to others, both socially and genitally. Broadening our understanding of sexuality necessitates that we also broaden our definition of sexual sin. We have already talked about the church's tendency to elevate sexual sins above others, and this is true, but it's usually a certain type of sexual sin, those of a genital nature. Our inconsistency is shown up again even within the area of sexuality. Addressing *only* genital sexual sins is not only inconsistent and puts an unfair burden on men, but it lets some very damaging social sexual sins off the hook! The magazines I just mentioned are a case in point. No one would blink an eye at a woman bringing a *Women's Day* into church, yet there would be an uproar if a man arrived with a *Playboy* under his arm! Aren't both types of magazines pornographic? I put women's magazines into the category of "social porn," because they can be just as damaging for women as "soft porn" can be for men. Think of all the faulty notions of beauty it breeds, the covetousness it generates, not to mention the gossip that ensues. These things surely can't be helpful for women, or men for that matter. Porn is porn, no matter what form it comes in.[21]

And what about sins around gender? Gender is fundamental to our sexuality, and yet we hardly challenge sins perpetuated on people's sense of gender identity or their unique expression of gender.

Many of these types of sins go under the radar in our homes and
churches; some are not even recognized as sins. When we broaden
our understanding of sexuality, we must broaden our understanding
of sexual sin and be consistent in what we call broken.

And finally, James Nelson reminds us that sin is not just in what
we might do with our sexuality, but is of a much more fundamental
nature:

> Actually, Christian theology at its best has recognized that sin
> is not fundamentally an act but rather the condition of alien-
> ation or estrangement out of which harmful acts may arise.
> However, it has taken a long time for theology to acknowledge
> that sexual sin is fundamentally alienation from our divinely
> intended sexuality.
>
> To put it overly simply but I hope accurately: sexual sin lies
> not in being too sexual, but in being not sexual enough—in
> the way God has intended us to be. Such alienation, indeed,
> usually leads to harmful acts, but the sin is rooted in the prior
> condition.[22]

It is this very sin, the failure to integrate sexuality into our lives
and the life of the church, that I am in part trying to address in
this book.

6. SEXUALITY IS DECEPTIVE

Frank Vilaasa, in his book *What Is Love? The Spiritual Purpose of
Relationships*, humorously helps us appreciate something of the
rather deceptive nature of romantic love:

> It is said that love is blind, and certainly in this state of ro-
> mantic love, we are temporarily blinded to any of the normal
> human frailties and shortcomings that our beloved may have.
> Or if we do see them we think they are part of the charm and
> are convinced that they are the nearest thing to perfection,

that they are "the one," and that this feeling of love will last forever. In fact, we are so convinced, that we start to re-schedule our whole future based on this new relationship. . . .

What we don't realize is that we've been drugged by nature. Romantic love is a bio-chemical trick that nature plays on us, in order to get us to reproduce. . . . Once nature has achieved its goal—once we have mated and (maybe) reproduced—the romantic love evaporates. The drug wears off, and we are thrown back into our normal state of perception. We look again at our beloved, and think "what did I ever see in you? What is that deformity on your chin?"[23]

Aside from his evolutionary assumptions about romantic love, there is an important truth being suggested here. The irony is that romantic love, despite the feelings of devastating certainty that ac-company it, is more likely to heighten one's capacity for deception, not lower it! When we get caught up in love's powerful hold, it's hard not to attribute what we are experiencing to a higher authority. C. S. Lewis cautions us of this:

Every human love, at its height, has a tendency to claim for itself a divine authority. Its voice tends to sound as if it were the will of God Himself. It tells us not to count the cost, it demands of us a total commitment, it attempts to override all other claims and insinuates that any action which is sincerely done "for love's sake" is thereby lawful and even meritorious.[24]

Who hasn't heard of a story where a pastor "falls in love" with someone on his/her staff, abandoning spouse and children to start a new life—leaving those in its wake both devastated and shocked, all the while justifying their actions—somehow making it all okay with God. Another example is a friend of mine who left her husband and children to run off with another woman (who also left a husband and children) because they fell "in love." Prior to this relationship neither of these women had ever been attracted to women before, and neither had believed that gay relationships were appropriate for God's people. Yet now that they had fallen in love they were convinced that God had led them every step of the way. My friend even reported that in embracing her "apparently latent" lesbianism she felt like she was being "born again" again!

> When one is in love, one always begins by deceiving one's self, and one always ends by deceiving others. That is what the world calls romance.
>
> Oscar Wilde

The reasons that events like these happen so often are in fact multifaceted and complex, but one must never dismiss the element of self- (and other) deception that is characteristic in almost all of them. Eros is by its very nature seductive; it allures by obscuring, by hiding, by deception. Being more ego-focused than the higher forms of love, erotic love is among other things an attempt to lure the person into an (eventually sexual) embrace. But it's not *just* romantic love, narrowly defined, that wields this type of power. Most of us have at some point experienced powerful nonromantic obsessions. These can happen with friends, a cause, a group of people or even someone quite distant from us, like that unreachable celebrity. Sexuality and attraction can be intoxicating (and they should be!), but as we noticed in the previous point, sexuality can only be experienced in and through our fractured, broken humanity. Our loves are flawed because we are flawed. Thus we can see that discerning our way through the various aspects of deception is tricky indeed, because it involves, among other things, negotiating some of our most hidden motivations. It also very much involves our belief systems and what we hold to as true and ultimately our sense of who God is. Most of us are either untrained or too busy to be really aware of these dimensions of life. Deception in a fallen world is woven into the very nature of things. And because sexuality is entwined all the way through our being, it should not surprise us that it would be a major battleground for either truth or deception, right or wrong, good and evil. Making right ethical choices when one is feeling the full force of attraction is not that easy. This is at the core of what the Bible calls temptation. The cost of obedience is felt most profoundly in these decisive moments. It is way easier for most of us to take the path of self-justification, rationalization and moral compromise. Joseph Agassi, in his confronting paper on deception says, "When one deceives oneself, one does not know the cost of self-deception, and it is usually this that makes the error significant."[25] The lie we embrace reinforces our deceptive thinking and keeps us captive to our addiction. Those who study the human mind and the interplay between the conscious and the unconscious have taught us much about the ways we as humans avoid uncomfortable reality. Psychological terms such as *denial, dissonance* and *rationalization*, all implying some form of self-delusion, have become part of the common parlance of our culture, and are more common in our lives than we would like to admit.[26]

Rationalizations lie at the root of our self-understanding and the image we project into the world—we do them all the time. No one lives without some dissonance, denial or rationalization. As it pertains to our sexuality, it seems some form of self-deception is part of the deal, which is why it is important to be aware of not only our own propensity to rationalize but sexuality's power to not only take us to the heights, but also to blind us. The truth is we all entertain a legion of little delusions.

Romantic and other forms of love can also be great gifts to us. They can lead us to truth as much as to falsehood. This double-

> Michael: "Don't knock rationalization. Where would we be without it? I don't know anyone who can get through the day without two or three juicy rationalizations. They're more important than sex."
> Sam: "Aw come on! Nothing's more important than sex."
> Michael: "Oh yeah? Have you ever gone a week without a rationalization?"
> Scene from *The Big Chill*[27]

possibility nature of sexuality is because it is directly related to our spirituality, our deepest longings to know and be known, and therefore needs to be discerned and directed toward holiness. Listen to Yancey:

> Romance gives intriguing hints of transcendence. I am "possessed" by the one I love. I think of her day and night, languish when she leaves me, perform brave deeds to impress her, revel in her attention, live for her, even die for her. I want to be both heroic and meek at the same time. For a time, and only for a time, I can live on that edge of exaltation. Then reality sets in, or boredom, betrayal, old age or death. I cannot sustain a state of complete absorption forever. At least, though, I can see in it a glimpse of God's infinite capacity for such attention. Could this be how God views us—views *me*?[28]

Romantic love ought to be dominant right at the beginning of relationships—in the courtship phase where attraction is most important—but it should not be the sole form of love in the end, or else that relationship is unlikely to go very far at all. And let's not forget that for many people romantic forms of love are seen as a Western privilege. There are many cultures where romantic love is not the indicator or predictive tool for marriage or courtship. We might look down on prearranged marriages and the like, but they *do* have very low divorce rates—perhaps there's a lesson for us here.[29] Covenantal love is our ultimate goal whether it be in our relationships or broader missional discipleship. I'm always saying to people that a romantic type of love might get them to the mission field, but only covenantal/sacrificial love will keep them there. Just like with marriage. Romantic love might get you down the aisle, but only the higher, more sacrificial love will carry you on till "death do us part."

Covenant love (*agape*) is the more holy, truthful, revelatory and self-giving form of love that *should* come to characterize our relationships. But it requires an abiding commitment to each other's best interests, to the ongoing search for truth, vulnerability, the risk of getting hurt and the accountability of our community.

7. SEXUALITY NEEDS A CHAPERONE

As we have seen, our sexuality certainly can, and does, get pretty messed up at times, not just in the area of romance and navigating desire, but in all our regular social interactions that make up our relational world. There is something in the nature of passion that drives us toward exclusivity. From the lover to whom we lose ourselves to the enemy we seek to do harm—each is some form of direct access that is not ours to have.

If anything needs a chaperone it's our sexuality. Whether it's sexuality's deceptive nature or our proneness to messing things up (relationally speaking), we need someone to stand between each of us, to represent us, to mediate for us—someone to remind us what right loving, right mercy and right justice look like.

In his book *The Cost of Discipleship* Dietrich Bonhoeffer talks at length about Jesus being the mediator between all of our relationships, not just the God-oriented one.

> We learn that in the most intimate relationships of life, in our kinship with father and mother, brothers and sisters, in married love, and in our duty to the community, direct relationships are impossible. Since the coming of Christ, his followers have no more immediate realities of their own, not in their family relationships nor in the ties with their nation nor in the relationships formed in the process of living. Between father and son, husband and wife, the individual and the nation, stands Christ the Mediator, whether they are able to recognize him or not. We cannot establish direct contact outside ourselves except through him, through his word, and through our following of him. To think otherwise is to deceive ourselves. . . .

There is no way from one person to another. However loving
and sympathetic we try to be, however sound our psychology,
however frank and open our behavior, we cannot penetrate the
incognito of the other man [or woman] for there are no direct
relationships, not even between soul and soul. Christ stands
between us, and we can only get into touch with our neighbors
through him.[30]

Simply stated this means that no person has direct access to another person. All access is in and through Jesus, our chaperone, so
to speak. That means Jesus stands between me and the one I am
relating to, filtering my image of them through the prism of himself
(see fig. 4.2). Loving God and loving others is not expressed without
our mediator guiding and correcting all our false, broken loves and
motivations.

As a counselor and minister for over twenty-five years, I can say
without a doubt that direct access to others is *not* helpful for us. Yet
it is exactly what our brokenness seeks. Christian tradition talks

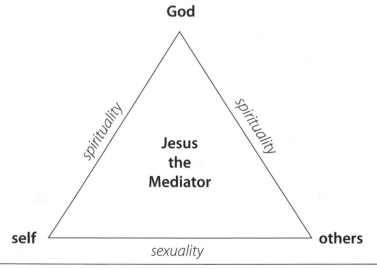

Figure 4.2. Jesus our mediator.

Gender Matters

Sex and gender are delicate subjects for church people.

JUSTIN TAYLOR

We have little information about what God originally intended in differentiating male and female, as we have spent eons since the creation re-creating ourselves in our own image.

S. L. JONES

Pink is for girls and blue for boys. Right? How would you respond if I told you that it used to be the opposite?[1] And that little boys wore dresses and didn't get their first hair cut till they were six or seven, and all clothing up until that age was considered gender neutral?

Documentation shows that back in 1918 the general rule was that pink was for boys and blue for girls. Pink, because it came from red, was thought to be a stronger color and therefore more suitable for boys. Blue was seen as more dainty and delicate, and therefore more appropriate for girls. The shift to pink for girls and blue for boys was established in the 1940s as a result of Americans' preferences interpreted by manufacturers and retailers, and could have quite easily gone the other way.[2]

This stayed the norm until the women's movement of the 1960s, where gender-neutral clothing was reintroduced. This remained (somewhat) popular till the mid-1980s, when prenatal testing allowed parents to prepare for the birth of their boy or girl. This of course was a marketer's dream, for the more you individualize clothing the more you sell. Since then pink and blue have been firmly established as gender specific—have you been to Toys"R"Us lately? This is the sheer power of advertising and marketing at work. Pink and blue are now entrenched gender categories and have become symbolic for a myriad of little adjectives and perceived psychological differences. Blue equals aggressive, nonrelational, strong, distant and so on. Pink equals soft, sensitive, frilly, emotional. Blue children are not allowed to cry; pink children are. Blue children can get dirty; pink children can't. And on it goes.

And the most tragic thing of all is that some (most?) kids will never fit neatly into one color.

WHOSE GENDER IS IT ANYWAY?

Gender (and identity) is a topic that has always fascinated me. Who we are as men and women, what roles we play and why, conversations around who says she does this and he that have been common for me. Yet I continue to find myself surprised, even shocked, at the lack of questioning within the church. For one, I'm a woman who doesn't like pink; I prefer hammers to aprons and like talking theology rather than baking.

In our home gender roles have always been up for grabs. Al and I tend to play according to preference and gifting rather than the typical stereotypes. That means Al does most of the cooking—because he's a better cook and loves it, and I'm definitely more the handy*wo*man. And I do the majority of the driving because he doesn't like it and I do. Now I happen to be married to someone whose masculinity isn't defined by these types of things. For us it's always been this way. We came into our marriage as a partnership of equals, appreciating and respecting each other's individuality rather than locking each other into restricting gender categories. And that's what this chapter is about.

So, who exactly determines who cooks or who builds? God? The church? Our biology? Our culture? Family of origin? Or do we ourselves decide? These are particularly hard questions to answer in any definitive sense. And I think this is why we (as a church) often resort to simplistic answers without appreciating the complexity of the issues at stake—not just theologically but pastorally.

> I left the church because I'm better at planning Bible studies than baby showers, . . . but they only wanted me to plan baby showers.
>
> **Rachel Held Evans**

WHAT IS GENDER?

When many of us think of the term *gender* we think of (biological) sex. And historically that was the case; the two terms were used interchangeably. But over time the two terms have become distinguished and more precise definitions given. The term *sex* (as a category) is now generally used to refer to a person's *biological sex* (i.e., male or female) and *gender* to the nonphysiological aspects of being male or female (i.e., the cultural expectations for femininity or masculinity).[3] Or as one author says, gender is "a social status based on the convincing performance of femininity or masculinity."[4] Despite this distinction, many of us continue to confuse the two, with gender thought to be the direct social manifestation of a person's biological sex.

Now to be fair, in most people it is extremely hard to cleanly separate the two—for they do overlap. Just how much is the question at hand. The key issues revolve around how we determine the degree that biological differences (as male and female) influence the development of a given gender. In other words, how much of what we do, how we think and how we behave is core to our nature (hardware) or our nurture (software).

There are two components to our gender sexuality: the *outside* face and the *inside* face.

Gender as the *outside* face we present to the world. Gender, our outside face, is what people first see of us. In all of our relationships we connect with people out of the gender we present. And the vast majority of us relate and are related to by the fact that we present as men or women.[5] I am seen and received as a woman, not a man. And in some way (for most of us) our gender is a reflection of and flows out from our biological sex. But for some people this is not the case. Take a transgender person for instance. Their biological sex might be male, but the gender they present to the world is in fact female (or vice versa). This constitutes a sharp discrepancy between one's biological sex and one's gender.[6]

Gender also includes our *inside* face. This has to do with how we *feel* about our gender. This relates to issues around what psychologists call our "gender identity"—a person's private sense of and subjective experience of their gender.[7] This is really about how we emotionally and psychologically navigate both the body we are born into and the gender characteristics and roles our culture commends.

For example, we can say that in any culture men *are* men (biologically speaking), yet what constitutes masculinity or manliness in a given culture is an entirely different issue. For what one culture deems *masculine* is not at all consistent throughout all cultures. For instance, Arab men hold hands when walking down a street, something that might invite all sorts of negative attention in Middle America. What is more, expressions of masculinity and femininity in any given culture can and do change over time. Every decade seems to create new expressions of what it means to be masculine or feminine.

LET'S GO BACK A BIT

For centuries it was assumed that the different characteristics of men and women (ideas and values about what constitutes masculinity and femininity), and the behaviors associated with them, were natural and immutable and determined by biological factors. For instance, women are meant to be more "naturally" nurturing because of the biological fact they can have children. In other words, a woman's biology determines the trait or characteristic. This characteristic is then associated with femininity, in this case "nurturing."

While no one argues whether men and women are biologically different, or that some of these differences impose certain limitations (e.g., men can't have babies), the question remains to what degree (if at all) should our biological differences determine our social roles within society. For instance, if men can't give birth to babies, does that necessarily mean they can't raise or nurture them? Now this logic might seem strange to some of us today where men are way more involved in parenting. But it helps explain why historically men have not been involved in child-rearing. In some cultures fathers didn't even see their children till they were seven years old.[8] Alternatively, just because a woman can give birth, does that mean she should *always* be at home and not have a career or job?

It's easy to see how our biology automatically equates with gender-specific roles when we look at how prehistoric society functioned. Many of the typical male and female roles were based around the need for women to be protected during pregnancy—which in those days constituted a large portion of her life. Being in such a vulnerable state created the perception that women were the weaker sex. And men were seen as stronger, given that they were not only the protector of women but the provider for the family.[9]

Over time, culture changes, and along with it the needs within a community. And with these changes comes a natural questioning of the assumed or outdated gender roles. Remember, they change all the time.

Theologian Stanley Grenz highlights this in relation to our modern Western context:

Women are not pregnant or nursing offspring for the greater part of their lives. Nor is a pregnant woman dependent on the physical strength of her husband for protection and suste-nance. In the same way brute strength has lost the importance for survival it once had. The significance of this change ought not be overlooked. As roles in procreation and nurturing of offspring lost their determinative influence over the wider social roles assumed by males and females, the door was opened to the assumption of new social functions for the sexes, especially for females, which in turn placed the tradi-tional gender roles under great strain.[10]

This strain is still evident in society today, where debate continues around how *different* men and women really are and how that im-pacts what roles they should have. And while researchers disagree on many points, one thing we can say is that while our biological sex is unchangeable, gender is certainly more dynamic and fluid.[11] And in fact "gender" (expressions of masculinity and femininity) can and does change from culture to culture, and is affected by caste, class, religion, ethnicity, age and other variables.[12]

A COMMON HUMANITY

Tim Kellis believes that "promoting the difference between people only promotes the underlying fear of those differences." The more different we think we are from others (be it sex, race, age, religion, etc.) the greater the potential for fear of the other develops, which easily lends itself to further alienation.[13]

Now don't get me wrong, as I state in chapter four, I do believe that men and women *are* different; otherwise what was the point of God making two sexes? But I believe first and foremost that we share a common humanity—and that makes us far more alike than different.

I like what philosopher and playwright Dorothy Sayers suggests:

perhaps men and women should be called "neighboring sexes" rather than "opposite sexes."[14] And perhaps we should begin to appreciate all the ways we reflect sameness rather than focusing on a myriad of perceived gender differences that may or may not be grounded in reality.

A fascinating example is given by Mary Stewart Van Leeuwen in her book *My Brother's Keeper*. Mary's colleague conducted a word association exercise with his students. He compiled a long list of adjectives, including the fruits of the Spirit: love, joy, patience, kindness, faithfulness, gentleness and self-control. He asked his students to rate them according to what was masculine and what was feminine. The results were to be expected. The fruits of the Spirit were largely classified as feminine, particularly the characteristics like "patient" and "gentle."[15]

Yet the fruits of the Spirit are surely gender neutral! Aren't they to be cultivated into the lives of *all* of God's people? They are *human* qualities. The implication? We all have the capacity to develop them, none are more natural to one sex or the other, and we are expected to allow the Spirit to grow these in each of us. As the old, pious Christian saying goes, "the fruits of the Spirit do not come in pink or blue!"[16]

This narrow scripting of assigning certain characteristics to boys and others to girls can do enormous damage to children who don't fit. What about little boys who are naturally more gentle? Are they to be seen as odd and unacceptable? And if so, why? And it seems that little boys get the bad end of the deal when it comes to navigating gender. Blue apparently has a narrower script than pink. In other words, little girls get to play in the blue playground more freely than little boys do in the pink one.

Regarding this, Van Leeuwen observes,

> Close to two-thirds of U.S. women report they were tomboys as children, and young tomboys, far from being ostracized, are usually popular with peers of both sexes. Boys, on the

other hand, are more narrowly socialized into the masculine
script, and the social costs of deviating from it are much
higher in terms of peer rejection and adult disapproval.[17]

I've had many parents talk to me about their more sensitive sons
who don't seem to like the "usual" boy things. Many think that
greater encouragement in "masculine" activities or buying them
more toy guns, trucks and the like is the answer. The problem is that
buying a truck for a kid who would rather paint or dress a doll can
lead him to further alienation from his masculine identity. Wouldn't
we do better to raise our kids according to their natural likes, gifts
and strengths, broadening out our own categories of gender in
order to accommodate them?

And make no mistake, there are some crazy and downright im-
moral ideas out there. A Baptist pastor in North Carolina came
under fire publicly when his sermon went viral. He was instructing
fathers how to deal with effeminate sons, "Dads, the second you see
your son dropping the limp wrist, you walk over there and crack
that wrist." He continued, "Man up, give them a good punch, OK.
'You're not going to act like that. You were made by God to be a
male and you're going to be a male.'"[18]

One of my favorite movies is *Billy Elliot*. The movie is set in
northern England during the coal miners' strike in 1984 and 1985.
Billy is an eleven-year-old and lives with his dad and older brother,
who are both miners, and they assume that Billy will simply follow
in their footsteps. One day Billy's dad sends him off to boxing
school—perceived to be a very manly activity. Billy dislikes boxing
but is forced to go. On his way to boxing school he happens upon
a dance class temporarily using the same building. He is intrigued
and eventually drawn into it, and ends up dancing instead of boxing,
all the while without his father's knowledge.

The story turns when the dad discovers Billy has been dancing
and not boxing. Things get heated, not just because Billy has been

deceptive, but because dancing is perceived as either a "girly" or "gay" thing. Billy's dad and brother are angry with him and also embarrassed. Dancing in their minds is definitely not seen as masculine and will never be acceptable in the harsh, exclusive masculinity of the mining pit. As the movie progresses we see this working-class dad struggle deeply to understand his son and to see him beyond his own limited view of masculinity.

This story has a happy ending. Both Billy's dad and brother take the difficult journey to embrace Billy's unique gifting and are able to expand their own vision of masculinity to include Billy's—who in the end becomes a famous, heterosexual dancer. But not all such stories have happy endings. In fact, quite the opposite.

When I worked as a counselor I heard time and time again awful tales of people being forced into the skewed gender stereotypes of parents, friends and churches—or risk rejection. I have even had pastors tell me they have restricted certain heterosexual guys from "platform" ministry because they were considered too effeminate, and by having them up front it might somehow be seen to be endorsing homosexual behavior! This is not only ignorant but deeply un-Christlike behavior! On its own skewed logic of cultural exclusion, Jesus would probably not make the worship team, crying and all in public as he had the tendency to do. And he was, after all, an unacceptable Jew who recruited the most unlikely, abnormal people to be the founders of his church.

> Every divergence deserves to be cherished, simply because it widens the bounds of life.
>
> Karel Capek,
> *Letters from Spain*

And where do people like Jasmine fit in? Jasmine is a transgender woman who "adopted" Al and me more than twenty years ago now.[19] She was born a boy but never really felt at home in her biological sex. From an early age she began dressing and identifying as female, culminating years later in her undergoing full sex-reassignment surgery. By all outward appearances

Jasmine is now a woman. People like Jasmine force us to face all our certainties about sex and gender, not to mention how we navigate this stuff both pastorally and practically in the context of the church. Insisting people like Jasmine simply return to the sex God made them is simplistic, to say the least. These are tough, complex issues that need to be navigated with sensitivity and loads of grace. People like Jasmine, who don't fit into the cultural gender stereotypes, already feel marginalized—they don't need church people reinforcing this.

I remember one young guy who came to our church. He was very effeminate yet dressed extremely conservatively. He had come from a high-conformity, culturally conservative church in our city. Over a couple of years of him being in a more accepting environment I saw him begin to blossom, not just with God but in his own self-acceptance and self-expression. It was like he was coming out of the cocoon of social conservatism and was able to expand his wings for the first time. He began dressing in the most creative and colorful outfits. To some his outward appearance might have suggested he was cultivating a "gay look," but it was *his* look. God was releasing him to be *him*! His creativity and artistic, even flamboyant, nature had been suppressed and forced to conform. This for him *was* liberation. What's wrong with colorful clothing after all?

And maybe this is the appropriate point to look to Jesus to see what we can glean about gender and expressions of masculinity.

GENDER JESUS STYLE

Over the years I have wondered about why God chose to reveal himself as a male. I've come to see that it's not the sex God was born into that matters but rather what we (both men and women) can learn about Jesus' security *in* and his expression *of* that particular sex. For God as the true man teaches us what it is to be a true human, and how important it is to subvert our own cultural expectations of gender when they are not in line with the model and work of his kingdom.

Those who attempt to butch Jesus up to try to make him more

marketable to "real men" are a case in point. Capitulating to cultural stereotypes of masculinity, they have in fact simply created a Jesus in their own idealized image. Yet the masculinity of Jesus defies our narrow categorizing. Is he a man, even a "real man" as some suggest? Well, yes and no. Yes, he is the warrior that confronts all that oppresses and the hero who saves the day, but he is also the servant who serves and the poet who weeps publicly and tells other guys how much he loves them. He is certainly a real *man* in every sense of the word, and if there is such a thing as "true" masculinity then it is surely found in Jesus. Yet it's not a masculinity that can be forced easily into narrow cultural scripts.

> "This man" has not been a failure yet, for nobody has ever been sane enough to try his way.
>
> **George Bernard Shaw**

Michael Frost, in his book *Longing for Love*, takes his readers on a journey through Jesus' life, exploring both his masculine and feminine sides. He looks at the temptations of Christ as just one example where we see a deep security displayed by Jesus in his masculine identity, where he both resists and subverts the cultural norms of how men would ordinarily express themselves in a Middle Eastern context.

In the first temptation Jesus is goaded by the devil to turn stones into bread. This is a classic instance, says Frost, when you might expect Jesus to abuse "masculine" power over objects for his own ends. Yet he resists. The second temptation is all about displaying flashy-type behavior. The devil challenges him to throw himself down from the highest point and order the angels to carry him to the ground. This exhibition would have certainly tapped right into the Jewish expectations of how the Messiah would appear, carried in by an angelic army. Yet again Jesus resists a macho-type performance. While certainly easy for him to do, it was not the image he wanted people to associate with the inauguration of his ministry.

In the third and final temptation we see Jesus being enticed with supreme political power. The devil promises him dominion over all the kingdoms of the world with all their splendor. Frost notes, "How classically masculine is it to hunger for universal control? For centuries men have fought for political domination, both nationally and internationally." Yet again Jesus resists, refusing to bow down to Satan or shortcut his ministry in order to get instant results. Frost writes:

[Jesus] refuses to allow his masculinity to be expressed in detrimental ways. Though decidedly masculine—though capable of controlling his environment, presenting himself dramatically and manipulating those around him for his own ends—Jesus refuses to express his sexuality in a negative way. It was his *animus* held in check by, or perfectly balanced with, his *anima*.[20]

There were many opportunities where Jesus could have overplayed the "masculine" card—and it would have been totally acceptable within his culture—yet he does not. The people of Israel had a clear view of the type of warrior-king they were expecting to liberate them. Yet from his incarnation throughout his ministry life and to the final surrender of his power on the cross, we see not some Rambo-style man ready to do some serious damage, but a man full of humility, who chooses instead to take on the form of a suffering servant.

Jesus not only modeled a new form of masculinity but seemed to go a step further by also actively and publicly displaying behavior and emotion that was seen as distinctly feminine. One example of this is when he ventures into what is normally seen as a domain reserved for women in Matthew 19. This is the story where Jesus allows the children to come to him. I always thought it a bit strange that the disciples would stop the children from coming to Jesus until I realized that children were not only seen as unimportant, they remained in the domain of the women; men really didn't get that involved. Yet here is Jesus—not really worrying about the cultural norms, he gives the children access to himself, dignifying them by giving them attention and blurring the barriers between the male and female domains.

Jesus is not afraid to express open and public displays of affection and emotion, including unashamed weeping when his friend Lazarus died. He is also unusually sensitive to the broken, compassionate toward the lost, feels grief and laments over Israel, and refers to himself as a mother hen when he cries, "Jerusalem, Jerusalem, . . . how often I have longed to gather your children together, as a hen gathers her chicks under her wings" (Matthew 23:37), a very clear image of maternal tenderness.

Again Frost observes,

[Jesus] is a perfectly whole human being who models what it looks like when an individual is able to integrate both the masculine and feminine aspects of his personality. It's true that he was born male, but he modeled such a sweet, perfectly balanced type of humanness that we can't but be impressed by his "femininity" as much as his masculinity.[21]

Jesus' relatively frank and open friendships with women are also worth mentioning again. As author Dorothy Sayers reflects,

[Women] had never known a man like this Man—there never has been such another. A prophet and teacher who never nagged at them, never flattered or coaxed or patronized; who never made arched jokes about them, . . . who rebuked without querulousness and praised without condescension, . . . who never mapped out their sphere for them, never urged them to be feminine or jeered at them for being female; who had no axe to grind and no uneasy male dignity to defend; who took them as he found them and was completely unselfconscious.[22]

Jesus both challenges and gives us permission to move beyond the cultural scripts of gender in our own time and culture. Tony Campolo reveals how much this has helped him in his own life to find a place of freedom and healing.

Not only do I love the feminine in Jesus, but the more I know

Jesus, the more I realize that Jesus loves the feminine in me. In a day and age when so many women are trying to rediscover the side of their humanity that the world deems masculine, I find Jesus is helping me to appreciate those dimensions of me the world calls feminine. . . . Society has brought me up to suppress the so-called feminine dimensions of my humanness. But when Jesus makes me whole, both sides of who I am meant to be will be fully realized. Then, and only then, will I be fully able to love Jesus and be fully able to accept His love for me. Until I accept the feminine in my humanness, there will be a part of me that cannot receive the Lord's love. And until I feel the feminine in Jesus, there is a part of Him with which I cannot identify.[23]

Jesus won't let his masculinity be stereotyped or let it be captive to fallen constructs. His is a masculinity in which all can and must be able to connect, regardless of sex or gender; all and every type of masculinity (and femininity) is held in his embrace.

6

Bi Now, Gay Later?

The Love that dare not speak its name.

OSCAR WILDE

I walked into the ladies' bathroom at a gay club I regularly frequented. I'm not sure why they bothered with the "Ladies" sign on the door, given that everyone walked freely in and out of either bathroom, as did I. Perhaps they kept the signs for the "straight" nights they also hosted, but back to the bathroom. . . .

I was standing in front of the mirror touching up my black lipstick (no longer my preferred shade). As I was attending to my face I saw a woman standing behind me off to my right, looking at me in the mirror. I kept her stare wondering what the issue was when she blurted out, "You're a lesbian, aren't you?" I was a little surprised and even humored—weren't we in a gay club? What was she expecting? But her words caught me strangely off-guard. I remember pausing and then as I looked back at my own reflection I heard myself saying, more to me than her, "Yes, I *am* a lesbian."

I knew at that moment—*really* knew. I wasn't playing a game like many others. The gay club scene was notorious for people hanging around who were unsure or exploring their sexuality. People probably just like that woman—who were curious—of us, of herself. The gay scene drew all types of people: gay, straight, bi, transgender, those questioning—everyone and anyone. It was a pretty inclusive scene.

Why am I telling you this? First, my knowing, or realization, like many others, points to the complex nature of human sexuality. And second, it raises a whole host of questions to do with orientation, behavior and identity, fluid or fixed sexuality, choice or not; these are important questions with life-impacting implications.

TO BE OR NOT TO BE?

The whole debate around whether sexual orientation is fixed or fluid, innate to who we are or something we choose, continues to rage. This is not just a debate between antigay and pro-gay groups, but even between members within the LGBT community itself.

Cynthia Nixon (from *Sex in the City*) created quite a stir when she announced to the *New York Times* that being a lesbian for her was a "choice." Nixon, who's been with her female partner for ten years, has not always identified as lesbian; in fact her previous partner was a man. Nixon's announcement was slammed by some of the more purists within the LGBT community. And it's not surprising, given the implications. Their point being that they have fought long and hard to be recognized as a "people" with rights. Much of the fight has been about this exact thing, whether gay people are choosing or not to be gay. The implication is that if being gay is a choice, then one can choose *not* to be. And this clearly has political implications.

Nixon eventually backed down and qualified her statement with something more in line with LGBT protocol, declaring instead that while she was choosing (at this stage in her life) to be with a woman, she was in fact born bisexual, and this *wasn't* something she chose but rather who she was. The problem for Nixon, and she declared this in her followup statement, was that many in the LGBT community don't fully embrace bisexuals. To these hardcore insiders, Nixon was now seen to be simply evading the issues by trying to hedge her bets both ways. You see, most people, gay and straight alike, prefer to believe that you are either gay or straight. Self-declared bisexuals create that gray space, and no one really knows what to do with them. They represent the *choice* word that makes many feel uncomfortable.

Either way, we need to ask the question of what *choice* really means in matters of sexuality. Certainly in my case choice did at times play a part in me identifying and living as a lesbian. Yet there were also clearly many things limiting my apparent freedom to choose, circumstances that conspired to push or orient me toward a certain direction. Some things didn't exactly feel like it was a matter of me ever choosing them.

FAMILY MATTERS

I remember on the night of my thirtieth birthday telling my mother and father for the first time about my lesbian background. I also told them about the abortion I had as a young woman. (Of course, this was all said from the safety of being married [to a man] and becoming a Christian.) It was like my big cathartic birthday gift to them. My poor parents. They knew that my sister and I had led some pretty wild lives, but there was a whole lot they didn't know—or even wanted to!

As I began to unveil my story, two things began to worry me—one was the look in my mother's eyes, and the other was the lack of response from my father. My dad finally broke his silence, and wobbling his hand from side to side like an unbalanced plane, said, "I always knew you were a bit [pause] you know."

I'm like, "You know *what*?"

"You know," he continued (hand still going), "a bit both ways."

I was the firstborn of four kids in a solid working-class family. My mother and father married young (as you did in those days) and went straight into having kids. Like most blue-collar workers, my dad tried his best to make ends meet. Mom worked as a local cashier.

Both had come from poor families and lived in government housing. When jobs were to be had, most were of the factory variety. My parents worked hard to lift us out of these realities, becoming the first in their respective families to buy their own home. This led some of our relatives to think of us as snobs. We weren't snobs; we just weren't in and out of prison like some of them.

My mother grew up not knowing where her next meal was coming from, and worked hard to make sure we didn't miss out on anything. And we didn't, except when it came to emotional nurture. We used to call our Nana (my mom's mom) the "Ice Queen"—and she was. It wasn't hard to see why Mom found it so hard to connect emotionally.

When I was a year old my first sister was born with a physical disability. This kept her in and out of the hospital for a number of years. Mom tells me that because of this I was often left to fend for myself as she attended to my sister. It's not surprising then that as a child I would follow aunts and older girls around seeking their attention.

When I was eight or nine I was abused by one of those older females. It literally took me years to acknowledge it as sexual abuse, partly because she never did anything sexual *to me*. But she did get me to do a lot *to her*. It was all part of the "game" we regularly played. These "games" opened me up to sexuality in a way I should never have known. And as they say, early sexual encounters leave a lasting imprint. It's not surprising that years later, in my first lesbian encounter, I was the one initiating the "grown up" games.

I met my first real best friend in secondary school, and she became my refuge. My emotional bonding with her was so intense that my mother became worried and one day confronted us. She came into my room and in a barely controlled voice asked, "Are you two lesbians?" The shock must have been evident on my face, because she became strangely quiet and backed out of my room, as if by giving voice to her fears she had somehow just set something in motion.

This was the first time I entertained there might be something unusually intense about my friendship. I was a kid; what did I know about the world of sexualized relationships? I just knew how I felt. This girl was my life and my soul—I couldn't imagine an existence without her. That old Peter Frampton song "I'm in you, you're in me" was our mantra.[1] And she was indeed *in* me, so much so that when another girl tried to get in on our little twosome, I gave her a black eye and bruised her face so bad that her mother ended up transferring her to another school!

The joke in our family was that if parents were allowed to have favorites, then we all knew who Dad's was. And I did have a special bond with my father—still do. Dads are particularly important in the life of their daughters because it's her first significant relationship with the opposite sex. And for better or worse it can have a powerful impact on the way she relates to men later on. Fathers play a formative role in affirming the gender identity in both girls and boys. Kids might more naturally role model off the relevant same-sex parent (if they are around), but dads will not only affirm the sense of masculinity in their sons but call forth the femininity in daughters.

My dad certainly did this for me. I never really struggled with my gender identity like some of my lesbian friends did. While I appeared strong and not overly girly (I didn't do the pink thing), I wasn't a tomboy either. I always *felt* like and saw myself as a female, although some of my close friends used to say that I wore my overalls on the inside!

Having a great relationship with my dad, an adorable younger brother, great uncles and the like, meant my early experience of men was pretty positive; that was until I had my first boyfriend. I was thirteen. He was a few years older than me, and when I think back now he was one damaged young man. I not only discovered the dark sides of male sexuality but became the recipient of his violence. I endured this physically and sexually abusive relationship for over two years, until I was brave enough to break up with him.

After this relationship ended I continued to date guys, but became increasingly aware of a deeper drawing to women (or was it a growing distaste for men?). I still had my best friend, but despite my mother's concerns, our relationship never became sexualized. It wasn't till I was sixteen that I initiated my first lesbian relationship, which continued on and off for about two years. I did still date the odd guy, but this all ended after getting pregnant and having an abortion at eighteen. At this point I can clearly remember washing my hands of men. I decided then that I would spend the rest of my life with a woman. And this is what I was doing several years later when Jesus found me—and I him.

Now one might wonder how much choice was involved in my own sense of being "gay." I clearly had an internal need to be with other women; did this make me gay? What about the fact that I also experienced heterosexual attraction? Was I bisexual? I certainly had a number of negative experiences with men that perhaps pushed me more into the gentler embrace of women. These are all complex questions and things to ponder. While I had been living openly as a lesbian woman by the time of my bathroom encounter, I clearly remember that night having a deep realization; it was like I fully and consciously embraced a gay identity.

IT'S ALL IN A NAME

Trying to understand or define homosexuality is no easy feat. One would be tempted to think that it simply means someone of a given sex being attracted (sexually or emotionally) to someone of the same sex. And in its simplest form this is true. But there are many variances and things to consider when trying to define and understand homosexuality. In fact it might be more accurate to say homosexuali*ties*.

For instance, when we talk about homosexuality we must be careful to distinguish between behavior, orientation and identity. Not all people who behave homosexually have a homosexual orientation. As odd as that might sound, consider situations where there might be only men or only women present (e.g., jail, the military, single-sex schools, etc.).[2] And not all who have a homosexual orientation identify or define themselves as gay. Those who do define themselves as gay may have different levels of same-sex attraction. That's why for some it's even more accurate to talk about attraction than orientation. And on it goes. And that doesn't include all the other relevant terms that make up the LGBT (QQII?) community.

When I say that it may be more accurate to talk about homosexual*ies*, as a plural rather than singular, I'm not saying anything new. But it is a very important distinction because not all who fall under the gay label experience their orientation in the same way. I have friends who would say that they are *exclusively* homosexual in their orientation. Others would prefer to call themselves *predominantly* homosexual; in other words, they experience some heterosexual response. But if you ask them whether they are more bisexual than homosexual, many would answer no because their heterosexual response is minimal.

And this is where the famous "Kinsey scale" comes into play. Sexologist Alfred Kinsey, back in 1948, developed a scale in an attempt to describe a person's sexual history or "episodes" of one's sexual activity at any given time—zero being someone who only and exclusively experiences heterosexual sexual activity, six being exclusively homosexual (see fig. 5.1).[3]

Kinsey was trying to show that we should be careful of simply categorizing people as either heterosexual or homosexual. These categories and labels are simply too rigid. His famous statement, related to male homosexuality, continues to resonate and inform even today, and it is well worth repeating given our propensity to box people:

> Males do not represent two discrete populations, heterosexual and homosexual. The world is not to be divided into sheep and goats. Not all things are black nor all things white. It is a fundamental of taxonomy that nature rarely deals with discrete

categories. Only the human mind invents categories and tries to force facts into separated pigeon-holes. The living world is a continuum in each and every one of its aspects. The sooner we learn this concerning human sexual behavior, the sooner we shall reach a sound understanding of the realities of sex.[4]

Kinsey's scale is old and might seem outdated, but I include it because it still continues to provide the base for all other scales. And while his scale focuses on behavior, other more comprehensive scales incorporate other aspects of one's sexuality and identity.[5]

Sexuality, like all aspects of our humanity, is simply way more complex and mysterious than we might first imagine.

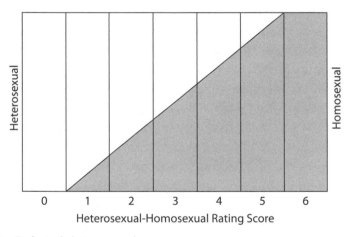

0 – Exclusively heterosexual

1 – Predominantly heterosexual, only incidentally homosexual

2 – Predominantly heterosexual, but more than incidentally homosexual

3 – Equally heterosexual and homosexual

4 – Predominantly homosexual, but more than incidentally heterosexual

5 – Predominantly homosexual, only incidentally heterosexual

6 – Exclusively homosexual

Figure 5.1. The Kinsey scale.

WILL THE REAL HOMOSEXUAL PLEASE STAND UP?

The *Baker Encyclopedia of Psychology* lists ten different types of homosexuality.[6] Most refer to heterosexuals involved in homosexual behavior, or to the adoption of homosexuality because of a given social role. For the purposes of this chapter I am only going to use two of the different types it lists. And I will take the liberty of expanding and developing each category as I understand and have experienced them. I have chosen these two because I am more familiar with these, and I believe they represent many of the individuals within the gay community—those that we ordinarily think of when we think of gay people. These are as follows.

Obligatory/definitive homosexuality. According to the *Baker Encyclopedia*, obligatory or definitive homosexuality occurs when an individual experiences an internal necessity to be with members of the same sex. In other words they can't seem to help it—and it certainly does *not* feel like a choice. This means that they didn't wake up one morning and think, *I'm going to thrill Mom and Dad to death today by choosing to become a homosexual.* For these individuals, as long as they can remember they have always been drawn to members of the same sex.

One of my closest male friends experiences this type of homosexuality. He can't remember a time when he didn't feel drawn to other males. If you asked him whether it was something he was choosing, he would laugh at you. In fact he would say that if he could have chosen not to be gay, he would have, since being gay has caused him so much grief.

He has experienced minimal heterosexual response with a couple of women throughout his life, but it's never been enough to enter into a relationship and live "happily ever after." He experiences his orientation toward men like the *Baker Encyclopedia* describes, as an "internal necessity," as simply the way he *is*.

It's interesting to me that in my experience, *almost all* of the men I know, and only *some* of the women I've known over the years, identify with this type of homosexuality. I have always thought that if research did uncover some genetic component to one's orientation, this would be the type it would be referring to, given that it is the most innate of all.

Preferential homosexuality. According to the *Baker Encyclopedia*, preferential homosexuality occurs when an individual is *preferring* to be with members of the same sex rather than the opposite sex. This type implies two things: first, that a person *can* be with someone of the opposite sex, and, second, that there is a degree of *choice* involved. But as mentioned earlier, choice is a funny thing. And while I get it that some people *prefer* to be with members of the same sex, for many it's just not a matter of simple choice; various factors seem to load the dice in favor of homosexuality in some way or another.

For a significant number of the lesbian women I know, this is the type of homosexuality they experience. Some would say *preferring* is too soft a word. It's more like they are *compelled* to be with other women—it's much stronger than simply making a singular choice. But many of these women would also admit to experiencing strong (and ongoing) heterosexual desire at different stages in their lives, which means this type of homosexuality isn't as innate as the previous type.

As in my own story, it is worth asking about just how much choice is involved. I may have made a myriad of little decisions over the course of time that headed me in a certain direction, but there were also other factors nudging me along, not to mention things I encountered that I had no choice in—a driving need for female love, strong bonding with other females, abusive relationships with men, and sexual abuse by a woman, to name a few. How much these things contributed or predisposed me to becoming a lesbian, it's really hard to say.

Whatever one thinks about the degree (or not) of choice, the general consensus (even from within the gay community) is that sexuality appears to be more fluid for many women than men. Cathy

Renna, a gay columnist and leader within the LGBT community, affirms this:

> I know plenty of women (including my wife) who may best be described as "lesbian-identified bisexuals," having the capacity to be attracted to men and women but choosing an identity that they feel comfortable with and which reflects how they want to be publicly known. How many? Who knows? And who cares? That's their choice, and I respect it. It is interesting how it seems more common in women than men, but that's a whole other post.[7]

This reflection squares with research conducted on the differences between male and female sexuality. Professor Roy Baumeister of Florida State University (and others) have shown that sexual attraction in many women seems to be more malleable than it does for men.[8] In other words, a woman's sexuality tends to be more fluid than a man's (see also chap. 4).

This has certainly been my experience, both personally as a young woman as well as professionally as a counselor and a pastor. This fluidity is not just evident with some of the gay women I know, but also with many other self-defined heterosexual young women who engage in lesbian relationships. This happens more regularly than most would imagine, inside as well as outside church circles. And it's not surprising when you think about it; women tend to be more socially, emotionally as well as physically engaged in their relationships with other women. They often share beds and are more physically demonstrable with each other than men are with other men (think back to social and genital sexuality). Therefore, for some women it's not that big of a step to engage (genitally) sexually with one another. Not to mention the subtle permission our culture gives to women to explore. Furthermore, lesbianism doesn't generate the same degree of social anxiety or even repulsion that male homosexuality tends to. In fact it has actually become culturally fashionable to be a lesbian (or at least dabble in it), as Katy Perry's "I Kissed a Girl" song demonstrated.[9]

There are also lesbian women who have never experienced heterosexual response that would fit into the "definitive" category. Longing for other women is all they have known and all they desire to know. And there are a myriad of categories in between on every point of the spectrum, and not just for the reasons I have already mentioned. For example, some prostitutes I've known over time have female partners, not necessarily because they experience innate homosexual desire but because for them men are seen as their "work," not their choice for partners.

Given that everyone's experience of sexuality is not only multifaceted but unique to their story, it's almost impossible to place a generic label on a whole group of people and think you've defined them. As anthropologist Jenell Williams Paris says, "Try to define 'gay' or 'straight,' and the words begin to slip through our fingers."[10] This complication with labeling raises the question of just how helpful these labels really are and whether they have outlived their usefulness. Paris suggests that they have, and challenges our reliance on contemporary Western paradigms that define the totality of a person.[11]

BORN GAY?

One doesn't have to search far to read the endless research and opinion as to why some people are homosexually oriented. Studies range from exploring genetics, the prenatal hormonal environment, brain structures, birth order, family dynamics and the like. Some theories stand in direct conflict with the other, some are helpful, some outright crazy! Yet none have been sufficiently established to produce any form of consensus. This means that at this point in time nobody *definitively* knows how or why homosexuality forms in the life of an individual. All we have are clues, not hard-and-fast rules. And just looking at the two (of the many) types of homosexuality, we can appreciate the impossibility of a one-size-fits-all approach.

Even if research does conclude at some point that there is some biological component, it will only ever be one piece of the puzzle, not the complete picture, perhaps enough to *predispose* one's orientation, not *predetermine*. In other words, it's not a determinative fact. An individual would have to have a whole host of other psychosocial factors working in line with the biological. This means there could potentially exist heterosexuals with genetic predispositions toward homosexuality, which never develops because of the lack of other influences.

No one is simply *born* gay. No surprises here. Lady Gaga is wrong. But it is certainly understandable that many who experience innate homosexual desire would hold on to the "born gay" theory—at least it *explains* why they feel this way.

The latest statement from the American Psychological Association affirms this complexity:

> There is no consensus among scientists about the exact reasons that an individual develops a heterosexual, bisexual, gay, or lesbian orientation. Although much research has examined the possible genetic, hormonal, developmental, social, and cultural influences on sexual orientation, no findings have emerged that permit scientists to conclude that sexual orientation is determined by any particular factor or factors. Many think that nature and nurture both play complex roles.[12]

Despite statements from the APA pointing toward multifaceted explanations for homosexuality, many mainstream gays and lesbians persist in turning to scientific explanations to validate their very existence. This is totally understandable given the degree of homophobia still present in our culture. Others in the LGBT community seek no justification and have mixed feelings about the whole genetics argument. Tracy Baim is one such activist:

I also do not believe we should base our quest for civil rights on an argument that we "can't help ourselves" because of our genes. This is a very dangerous and slippery slope. There have been fictional books and films made about this topic: if there is a gay gene, should it be eliminated, or a child aborted, if it's found? Science fiction isn't usually far removed from science.[13]

DOES IT REALLY MATTER?

Knowing *why* doesn't seem to be the top priority of gay politics as it once was, given that knowing could prove to be a double-edged sword. But gay people, like all people, just want to be recognized and accepted for who they experience themselves to be, despite the degree of choice or not involved in their lifestyles. It is a profoundly *human* issue, and followers of the incarnate God ought to be very sensitive to this.

This is a great challenge for the church in our time. It might even become a defining one. But it should not be so. How do we move from vitriolic polemics to the love that we are commanded to show to a love-starved world? How do we represent Jesus to a group of people who have largely written off the church? I remember reading a survey that was taken among members of the LGBT community in San Francisco. They were asked a series of questions about what the factors were that kept them actively involved in their community. The top two answers were *acceptance* and *belonging*. Acceptance because they were not judged for being different. And belonging, because many had been rejected by their families and church communities. The LGBT community had literally become their new home.

Acceptance and belonging. Do these sound familiar? They should to all people seeking to find God in the midst of life. And they ought to be two features that mark the church of Jesus Christ. But unfortunately we don't deal with differentness all that well in the church.

And the evidence of this has certainly been felt by our gay brothers and sisters, not just in our lack of understanding them but in our attempts to try to make them become "normal" (i.e., straight). And this is what chapter seven will deal with.

7

Limping Straight to Heaven

When I lay these questions before God I get no answer. But rather a special sort of "No answer." It is not the locked door. It is more like a silent, certainly not uncompassionate, gaze. As though He shook His head not in refusal but waiving the question. Like, "Peace, child; you don't understand."

C. S. LEWIS

And am I not, Master of the Universe, Thy child? Yet I do not beseech Thee to reveal to me the mysteries of Thy way; I could not endure them. But this I pray Thee to reveal to me, deeply and clearly, what this thing that now happens means to me, what it demands of me, and what Thou, Master of the Universe, wouldst communicate to me through it. Ah, I need not know why I suffer, only whether I suffer for Thy sake!

R. LEVI ISAAC OF BERDICHEV

My sister Sharon was born with a deformed leg. Well, she tells me that the politically correct term is "differently abled." But it looked pretty messed up to me. She had one good, "normal" leg;

the other one was about a third the length, with a foot minus a heel that sort of hooked upwards with three toes. She used to call that foot Freddie. They had to make some weird contraption for Freddie so she could walk. But there was no hiding him; it was pretty obvious to all who saw my sister that she had a deformity. Freddie remained part of her life until she was twelve, when he was amputated to make way for her new prosthetic leg.

We used to have a lot of fun with that prosthetic leg—appropriately named George. I remember once in our wilder days when we were stoned and up to mischief, we turned the foot around so the shoe pointed in the opposite direction, then went into McDonald's. We loved watching people's reactions. She would take that leg off and leave it in the strangest of places—all for shock value. It also came in pretty handy as a weapon when needed against me and our other siblings.

Putting all the fun aside, I struggled with her leg. This was my sister. I didn't want her to suffer, to stand out. But she did. My early memories are plagued with the ridicule hurled upon her, not to mention the fights I would get in on her behalf. I loved my sister and just wanted her to be "normal," like the rest of us. But she wasn't, she couldn't help it—she was born that way. And being born different in this world is never easy.

As a young believer my sister was invited to attend a healing ministry where a number of well-meaning people prayed for her leg to grow back. They even marked the place where her stump came up to on her other leg so she could keep track of God's healing work. She went to bed for weeks with the anticipation that God could and would grow her leg back. But it never did grow. When well-meaning Christians assert healing as a birthright of the Christian to be fully experienced *now*, and it isn't, it can have all kinds of negative ramifications for the individual. It certainly did with my sister, creating all sorts of doubt and confusion to eat away at her newfound faith.

My sister's story, though specifically related to her birth defect, nonetheless provides us with a mirror with which to understand all our stories and our search for wholeness and redemption. What does it mean for Sharon, or for any of us, to be made whole? What can we legitimately expect from God in the form of healing and hope? To what degree do we have to struggle with ongoing brokenness in a still-broken world? And how are we to understand such things? Should my sister (or any of us for that matter) expect God to heal her? What does healing this side of heaven even look like? And for the purposes of this chapter, how do we understand and navigate these realities as they pertain to sexuality and sexual redemption?

STRAIGHT FORWARD?

In the early years of our pastoral ministry our church attracted many people who experienced some form of homosexual orientation—at one point accounting for as much as 40 percent of the people in our church. Many had come from the LGBT community; others had grown up in the church. No matter where they came from, they came looking for answers—from us, from the church and ultimately from God. Many were asking whether they could be free from unwanted homosexual desires.

As a church community we were hopeful for change, for both gay and straight alike. We saw heterosexuals as no less broken (and in need of salvation) than homosexuals. We were all together in the human experience of life and trying to live out the reality of the kingdom. We even changed the name of our church to include the words "Restoration Community," believing that God was in the business of restoring *all* people—slowly but surely transforming each of us into the image of his Son.

At the time (back in the early 1990s) we became associated with (and eventually took over the leadership of) a local Exodus International ministry that was operating in our city. These people seemed to understand the particular issues related to homosexuality, and we found a place with them. Over time however we became increasingly uncomfortable with some of the literature being produced by the larger Exodus ministry. Some of the claims they were making—particularly as it related to what healing looked like, and what one could realistically expect from God—didn't equate to what we were seeing.

Before we officially parted ways with Exodus, I brought our concerns to one of the Exodus International leaders, explaining that our ministry experience was at odds with some of their teaching, and I asked for theological justification for their views. The leader stated quite simply that they believed that in Christ one *could* experience what was a true "biblical sexuality" (i.e., heterosexuality). And in Jesus one *could* return to God's original intent.

The problem for us was that our own stories simply did not bear witness to this. We understood the complexities of human sexuality, and knew that people experienced homosexuality differently. Mark's and my own story were two cases in point. By this stage in my journey I had married Al and started my own walk back to a lost (and what was a pretty damaged) heterosexuality. This was not the case for others; some had never even experienced heterosexuality. Where did their hope lie? How much could or should they expect from God? They were not "returning" to a lost heterosexuality— they never had one to begin with.

Based on the logic of Exodus, *in* Jesus my sister (and anybody else with one leg) should be able to return to God's original intention (i.e., grow another leg). If we can make a case for a biblical *sexuality*, then we should be able to make a case for a biblical *physicality*. Why would we believe in one and not the other?

Now I know sexuality is a little more complex than that, and many people can and do experience healing on a whole host of levels. I certainly have! But the point I'm making is that for an individual to move from being *exclusively* homosexual in their orientation to becoming *exclusively* heterosexual would mean God has worked a major miracle, something akin to growing my sister's leg back. And I just have to be honest and say that even after so many years of ministry, I personally have never met such an individual.[1] Not that I don't believe God can perform miracles, God is God after all! I've just never personally seen it happen.

And let me immediately add that similarly I've never met a heterosexual who has been *fully* healed and still doesn't struggle in some way with his or her sexuality. Just because a heterosexual orientation (in direction) might appear to be closer to God's original intent, it's by no means flawless. In fact, if we were equally honest we can probably say that most male heterosexuals are actually polygamous in orientation; in other words, their "natural" preference is for many sexual partners, not just one, which is clearly not what God would have originally intended. Every human being on the planet is sexually broken. Everybody's orientation is disoriented. *All* of us are on a journey toward wholeness; not one of us is excluded.

NO MORE TEARS?

Cleary this raises larger difficult issues about the universal human struggle with real brokenness, estrangement, evil and sin. These are existential issues that *every* human deals with in concrete, day-to-day, lived life. No one is born whole or even achieves complete wholeness in this life. The proof of this is that everyone reading this book will one day die. And there is not a person alive who doesn't struggle with a long-term illness, disability, systemic dysfunction, addictive behavior or the like. And there is not one of us who doesn't desire to be healed, able-bodied or free. Only the most self-deluded (or self-righteous) person could say that he or she is, or always has been, completely whole. We are all on a journey to that end.

The way the Bible says that these issues are resolved is encapsulated in the term *salvation* or perhaps even more specifically *redemption*. What does it mean to be saved? How does this relate to my distinctive story, my particular life? And when it comes to aspects of psychology, what does redemption mean for all forms of broken sexuality? What is wholeness, and what is the possibility of wholeness? What can legitimately be hoped for?

I have to admit that these issues are complex and beyond my finite understanding, but there are some things that I do know that must factor into this. First, I *do* know that Jesus really does save us—I know it personally and have seen it universally. I also know my Savior was and is a healer of people. He did it all the time in his ministry. When he healed, it was always an aspect of God's mercy and a sign of the inbreaking kingdom of God. Healing therefore has a very close association with salvation. And interestingly the root word for salvation (*sōzō*) is also the root word for healing—the one is implied in the other. Salvation is real and is found in some mysterious combination of the redeeming work of Jesus on my behalf, the experience of eternal life right now, the power of the indwelling Spirit, the invading presence of the kingdom and the yearning for the return of our Savior-King, when all our hopes will be fulfilled. The salvation we experience in Jesus involves the reality of a God-filled, meaningful life, and along with that the promise of full human restoration and healing.

But I am also all too aware that this reality of salvation/healing is not yet fully complete and requires a future action on God's part to bring it to its true end. We live in what has been called the *now* and the *not yet*. We *are* saved but we are also *being* saved (Philippians 2:12). The same, therefore, is true for our healing. We all know that even if God does heal me from a cancer, this current body will still eventually expire. In other words, our healing in Christ is real, but in this now-and-not-yet world we live in, it is only experienced in anticipation of the complete and final redemption. Healing is therefore a proleptic sign of the kingdom to come, where there will be no more tears, no more sickness and brokenness, and all the redeemed will live in the unmediated presence of God. To trust Jesus as Savior is the heart of our faith, and to anticipate final redemption is already to have experienced some of that full salvation that is to come. The hard

thing is to live in the tension of the now and not yet. How we negotiate this tension defines our lives in so many ways.

I also know that to be saved we have to know what it means to
turn to him in repentance, with all our broken parts, to reorient
our lives toward God and his kingdom. And this means accepting
the logic of the biblical narrative about our waywardness and
transgression. Repentance involves accepting our broken condition and looking to the Savior Jesus to fill our gaps. We can't have
it on our own terms; we have to accept God's perspective on the
human condition. This calls for humility and self-surrender. There
is no room for any self-justification.
Every human being must turn toward
God in this way. This is important because, first, it applies to all of us, and,
second, it means aligning ourselves with
God's purposes and designs.

This is true for sexuality, as it is true for
any other aspect of our humanity. This is
true for heterosexuals, as it is for homosexuals, bisexuals, transgender people and
the like. We all must turn, with all that we
are (sexuality included), in order to receive
saving grace. No one is excluded from this
call, and there is certainly absolutely no
room for self-righteousness, because we
are *all*—at the end of the day and to the
end of time—beggars showing the other
beggars where to get the bread. Only when
Jesus returns shall we be perfect in our hu-
manity; until then we keep pressing on to become like him. Sanctification and maturity is a process that culminates in the return of Jesus.
Until then, we *all* need to live with some level of incompleteness and
brokenness. None of us escape that!

> I press on to take hold of
> that for which Christ
> Jesus took hold of me.
> Brothers and sisters, I do
> not consider myself yet
> to have taken hold of it.
> But one thing I do:
> Forgetting what is behind
> and straining toward
> what is ahead, I press
> on toward the goal to
> win the prize for which
> God has called me
> heavenward in
> Christ Jesus.
>
> **Philippians 3:12-14**

The Bible doesn't give us all the answers to the questions raised in Sharon's story, but I do know that our God is a good God, and that one day we *will* understand. We will get an eternal perspective of the particular limp we walk with through this life. Just like other saints throughout history, everyone has to navigate their particular brokenness, their particular pain. The question is not whether we will experience pain. The question is whether we allow it to bring us to the foot of the cross. Whether we are willing to enter into the mystery that suffering and sanctification weave together.

ROADS TO JESUS

My dear friend Richard allowed his pain to bring him to the foot of the cross, and in doing so he has become a modern-day saint. As a young gay man he lived a pretty reckless life of sex and drugs, and even worked as a male prostitute for a while. Then he encountered Jesus. His life was radically turned around. He went off to church and began to pursue God with great passion. I've wondered whether Richard would even be alive today if it wasn't for Jesus.

Richard eventually met a woman at his church that he was drawn to. He pursued her, and when it became more serious he sought the counsel of his pastor as to whether he should tell her about his background. He was advised not to. It wasn't considered necessary because he was a "new creation" and all that stuff was "under the blood of Jesus." Richard took his pastor's counsel and eventually married this woman without telling her about his background—probably not the best way to start a marriage! But eventually he did tell her some of his story, and then after they had their first child things began to somewhat unravel. Richard started to recall painful memories of sexual abuse from his childhood.

Part of the problem for Richard was that he hadn't dealt with any of his past. When he found Jesus he literally put it all behind him, and his church encouraged this. But things eventually catch up with us. Richard didn't end up using heroin and selling his body because of some idyllic childhood! And some of these things were surfacing and now demanding his attention. At this point Richard embarked on probably one of the most soul-searching and difficult periods of his life.

As Richard entered this season, what we might call his "dark night of the soul" time, he realized one of the things he had to face was that his homosexual desires hadn't completely left him. Apparently the gospel doesn't involve God simply obliterating our history. God is a redeemer not an eraser. Our past, in some way, will always be with us, always a part of who we are and have become, an inextricable part of our life narrative. It can be redeemed but not erased. Or as C. S. Lewis so aptly describes, "Humanity does not pass through phases like a train passes through stations: being alive, it has the privilege of always moving forward but never really leaving anything behind. Whatever we have been in some sense we are still."[2] Part of Richard's healing came in the acknowledgment of this, not in the denial. He had to learn how to integrate this part of his sexuality into the totality of who he was, while maintaining faithfulness to God and his family.

Richard told me that as he began to do this, he discovered that part of his attraction toward some men was based on his own deep insecurity within his masculine identity. Was he athletic enough? Did he demonstrate the qualities of masculinity based on his career or social group, or even within his Christian community? Given that he'd also been sexually abused as a child, his understanding of sex had also been very badly damaged. As he began to understand his own sense of masculine identity and deal with his particular insecurities, Richard slowly started to feel more comfortable in his own skin as an integrated man, husband and father.

Some might think that Richard wasn't being true to himself because he chose not to live according to his same-sex feelings. He doesn't see it that way. Despite (or perhaps because of) his "dark night of the soul" experience, he now says he's never lived such depth of life or experienced such great joy with God and his family as he does now.

In fact, his sexual relationship with his wife has been a rich and deeply fulfilling journey for them both—far outweighing his previous experiences prior to knowing Christ. If you met Richard you would see, like I see, the depth of love and inner peace he has. Not because he avoided the hard stuff but because he faced it. His journey hasn't always been easy and isn't complete, but he has, with God's help, made a new life for himself—one he never dreamed he could have.

I don't know about you, but my story was a little like Richard's. When I came to the Lord I sailed for a number of years basking in my newfound faith, not really considering the impact of some of my own early sexual abuse. I honestly didn't think it was an ongoing issue. And perhaps that was simply God's grace given to me for a season, especially as a new believer trying to negotiate a new way of life. But then the time came when he needed to take me to deeper places, and to do this meant dealing with a number of different issues. I suspect the same is true for all of us. We need to appropriate God's grace at deeper levels as we go in order to mature as a person as well as a lover of God.

THE NEW NORMAL(?) ROAD

In his insightful book *Addiction and Grace*, Gerald May observes that humans are the most adaptable creatures in God's creation, and have the capacity to constantly create new normalities for ourselves.[3] I believe that he is right. All of us, like Richard, have the potential to live lives we never thought were possible. This doesn't mean we move forward ignorant of our past. Our history *is* part of our story. But we can live *beyond* that history, beyond how we might feel in the present, on into a new tomorrow. That is the promise of God.

I could tell you story after story of people like Richard who *are* living lives they never thought they could. Men and women who are married (to the opposite sex) who have or are raising children and loving their lives. These individuals are not in denial about their sexuality; they are simply choosing *not* to live according to one aspect of it. They are making new paths or new "normalities" for themselves with God's help.

Many people ask me what my journey was like. And I say that learning to love a man wasn't really the issue—intimacy was. I had to learn to trust a man again in those tender areas where trust, or perhaps even the possibility of trust, had been broken. And to be honest, at first even the thought of having sex with a man gave me a sense of revulsion. It took me a long time and a loving, patient husband. But I was, as mentioned, returning to something I had lost. Others, like Richard, have had to learn completely new experiences, heterosexuality being one of those.

I remember a now-married man describing how being intimate with the opposite sex felt. Initially at least, he said it was like walking around with his shoes on the wrong feet. It felt strange and not quite "normal." And that's because it wasn't normal to him, at least at the beginning. But because it was something he wanted to do, he kept walking forward. Over time he began to feel more comfortable and confident, and declared, "Well, I guess heterosexuals also have to learn how to be intimate—it's scary for all of us!"

Others have found it a little easier, perhaps like going to another country where you have to learn to drive on the other side of the road—an experience I know only too well after moving to America! At first it can be pretty strange, but it becomes more natural the longer you drive. As Gerald May says, we can all learn new things. But we can also return to the old country and to old ways, especially if they feel more natural to us, just like driving on the other side of the road.

Now these clearly are mere analogies and ought not be pushed too far. But the point is that people can adapt and change their behaviors, and for some maybe it does, over time, even impact their orientation. For many, though, their "freedom" is not seen as much in "losing" their homosexual orientation as it is about wanting to learn to grow and develop heterosexually.

I had a conversation recently with someone I know really well.

Prior to his marriage he would have called himself exclusively homosexual. He has now been married to a woman for ten years, and he told me that while he still has a gay orientation, he feels that he has definitely developed heterosexually and that he enjoys having sex with his wife, and his body has learned to respond to her touch. He said he doesn't feel attraction to other women as he does with his wife, but he is glad he doesn't, claiming he doesn't want to be *that* heterosexual!

Now I know we all have to be very careful with this "change is possible" type stuff. This is, after all, why our particular ministry left Exodus all those years ago, and why Exodus International recently closed down its own ministry doors.[4] When you base "change" on a faulty premise, you have no solid platform from which to engage an authentic future. And no ministry or church has the right to impose any change on an individual, let alone one so intrinsic as a sexual orientation. But every individual must be given every opportunity, with eyes wide open to all the information (and there is now plenty of that!), to choose the unique path he or she wants to go. This is the same for an individual wanting to explore a heterosexual relationship as it is for one choosing to engage in a gay relationship. God gives each of us a free will that ought not be violated.

These particular stories of those choosing to explore heterosexual relationships are clearly not everyone's story. And they are only representative of some homosexually oriented individuals. Many of those who have a homosexual orientation will not (or have no interest to) pursue a heterosexual relationship. And we will come back to them.

But first a word of caution.

The stories of individuals who have begun to pursue heterosexual sexual expression have, over time, been showcased and used as weapons in various political agendas, individual and organizational. We certainly experienced this in our early years, right-wing political organizations wanting to interview people to see how straight they had become, all to prove that homosexuality is after all a choice and that gay people can and must be healed. I continue to find instrumental use of people as ideological agenda an appalling violation of people's rights. And to be sure, this goes both ways of the political divide.

Both the church and broader society are guilty of this. Both have made some profound mistakes, not just politically but therapeutically.[5] Not to mention directly (or indirectly) cultivating a culture where heterosexuality is seen as the norm, something to be aspired to, making those who are not heterosexual feel at best like second-rate citizens, and at worst like reprobates, never being able to live up to God's standards. And if we follow this logic, if gays can become straight, that means straights can become gays, but those who celebrate gays becoming straight do not think the opposite can be true or celebrated.

THE CELIBATE ROAD

Not all gay people who follow Jesus either want or feel able to explore the possibilities of heterosexuality. Many of my same-sex attracted friends have no inclination to be married to the opposite sex. Instead, they are choosing the path of celibacy as the way of faithfulness. It should be acknowledged that in a profoundly sex-oriented culture this can be a difficult path to tread. Which is why we must, once again, point back to Jesus, the one who provides the model for what a healthy sexual celibate looks like!

Let me reiterate, to be celibate doesn't mean a person must repress his or her sexuality or become a hermit. Quite the opposite. There is a world of social sexuality that legitimately can be explored (see chaps. 3-4), where one can discover richness and depth in a huge array of possible relationships (see chap. 11). Some of the most saintly people I know personally, and certainly many throughout history, have taken the path of celibacy. The apostle Paul spoke of the benefits, and Jesus himself lived as a celibate man. We must also remember that celibacy is not exclusive to homosexually oriented disciples but also to the heterosexually oriented single person who will not marry.

As I mentioned in the Jesus chapter, we need to take a fresh look again at celibacy; it's not the spooky monster it's made out to be.

THE OKAY-WITH-GAY ROAD

There is, of course, another road that homosexually oriented people can choose, and that's seeking to live in a monogamous same-sex relationship. I have many friends who are walking this path and would find no incompatibility with their relationship and following Jesus. These friends assert among other things that the Scriptures do not address a modern-day understanding of homosexuality, and therefore they do not apply to them. They feel free to fully integrate their sexual orientation and identity into their Christian spirituality. They believe "God is okay with gay," not just with their orientation but behavior as well. This is certainly a growing movement among confessing Christians. Many holding these views attend gay churches such as the Metropolitan Community Church, while others opt for more mainline churches who are both "welcoming and affirming." And while there has been a significant shift in evangelical churches with "welcoming" LGBT people, there is still lots to be processed and discussed related to what it means to "affirm" lifestyle choices that may run contrary to deeply held theological beliefs. But it seems to me that there is definitely a softening of some of the harder edges in many of the gospel-centric churches across the country.

Justin Lee, founder of the Gay Christian Network (gaychristian .net) has become something of a representative for young gay Christians exploring what it means to be gay and Christian. The organization, made up of side A and side B ("A" supporting same-sex marriage and relationships; "B" promoting celibacy for Christians with same-sex attraction), is doing much to further the dialogue between the two views, with Justin himself representing side A. They are attempting to model what healthy dialogue looks like among diverse opinions. The church as a whole could learn from them.

> For lots of people, the real problem is not sex but the loss of healthy community.
>
> Howard Snyder,
> *Homosexuality and the Church*

These are not the only paths people are walking. Some choose to be in what might be called "companion relationships," where a couple might live and share life together, supporting one another in a myriad of ways, yet they are not erotically or even necessarily romantically involved with one another. I've also met a couple of women who have embraced a gay identity, got officially married and now share a home together. They live just like any other married couple, except that they feel God has called them to be celibate in their marriage! There seem to be all sorts of ways people seek to fill their relational and sexual needs.

As Wendy Vanderwal-Gritter says in her book *Generous Spaciousness*,

> Regardless of biological sex or sense of gender, human beings (as image bearers of their creator) fulfill the drive to overcome their aloneness in a variety of creative, relational ways. As relational beings, they have the opportunity to experience various levels of intimacy (including emotional, spiritual, and physical) manifested in a variety of relationships: a monogamous covenant relationship, long-term friendships, a member in a community, a member in an extended family, and so on.[6]

People simply need people. And as difficult as some of these relationships might be for many conservative evangelicals to accept, the question that needs to be dealt with here goes to the issue of how we can all be redeemed members of God's family and yet disagree on occasion. Are the people who choose this path still brothers and sisters? Surely the answer must come from the claim to have the same Father in and through the saving work of Jesus.

And that answer must be based on their confession and the work of God in their lives, just like the rest of us. Once again, it is worth saying here that all of us hobble into heaven and get there by grace. There is no room for self-righteousness and exclusion based on disputed interpretations on nonessential issues of the Bible. I like the way theologian Howard Snyder distinguishes between a *core* issue (one that contains complex theological and ethical implications) and what he calls an *essential* one.

> By *core issue* I mean that one's position on homosexual practice involves a set of assumptions about biblical authority and about salvation that are critical to Christian faith and practice. The integrity of our faith is involved, in both doctrine and behavior (which are, at heart, one). . . . And yet the biblical proscription of homosexual practice is not itself an essential doctrine. This is true for two reasons. First, neither the Bible nor the church's historic creeds deal explicitly with the issue. Second, biblical teachings on salvation, and specifically on justification by faith, ground salvation fundamentally in God's grace, not our behavior.[7]

While this does not lessen the importance of the scriptural witness, it does help us to keep perspective. The issue of affirming gay monogamy does not qualify for the same authority as issues relating to the Trinity and the resurrection (see chap. 11 on the church as well). If it did, then we would have to put many other things that we all do on the table as well. And let's be honest, most of us would not want that, because it would not be pretty!

The church has certainly come a long way in its understanding of the homosexually oriented person. Ministries set up to in effect make gay people straight are becoming increasingly rare and more marginal. Organizations like Exodus International have now shut down; other ministries have shifted their focus from orientation change to broader discipleship and holiness models, recognizing that the opposite of homosexuality is not heterosexuality. And there are now many different paths that people are walking in order to not only make sense of their sexuality but to be able to express it in ways they feel are life-giving for them.

Perhaps we all need to develop what Wendy Vanderwal-Gritter calls a "generous spaciousness":

> The point is not to call for a watered-down discipleship. The point is we all need generous spaciousness in our walk with Christ. We all need room to live in the tension of the call to virtue and the longing for happiness. And we all need to find safety and grace in our friendships and community so that we don't have to try figure this out alone. The truth is, different people with different personalities, backgrounds, experiences, and capacities will navigate this paradox differently. The amazing good news of the gospel is that God is rich in grace and lavish in mercy. He knows us by name, he counts the hairs on our head, he knows our weaknesses and our strengths, he knows our frame and that we are dust, and he knows our heart. In him we are set free from striving, set free from being motivated by fear, guilt and shame. In him we can find rest.[8]

8

Uncomfortable
Sex Positions

Truth survives because real holiness is irresistible; it exercises a strange and compelling power over the hearts of men and women.

JOHN HENRY NEWMAN

I spent several hours in the course of writing this book talking to a good friend of mine. He is an amazing guy and one of the best missionaries I know. I love him and value his opinion on many issues of life, including theology, politics, the arts and beyond. My friend deeply loves God—and the way he loves his family, his neighbors and God's Word are a testament to this. His daughter, who is a devout follower of Jesus, recently told him she is gay.

When we love someone we'd give our lives for, and they declare they are gay, it's like *everything* changes. All the opinions we had, prejudicial or not, are challenged and reassessed. Homosexuality becomes personal, no longer "out there," associated with "those people"—it invades our lives, and it's here to stay.

Where one now positions him- or herself, theologically speaking, becomes an intensely personal issue. And while it might seem more clear-cut when our son or daughter is not following the ways of

Jesus, it's another matter when they are. Things once previously accepted at face value are now put under the microscope. What does God really think about this? How does this relate to my son or daughter, my friend or work colleague? Silent doubts and heartfelt confusion begin to creep in.

My friend is not alone. We all know someone. If it's not a family member, it's a friend or a friend of a friend, or a work colleague, or *someone*. And for a growing number of us, it's our neighbors—the people who live right next door! For those of us trying to work out what we think God thinks, and what we think about what we think God thinks (and there is a difference!), it's hard enough, let alone being able to communicate this to someone who *is* gay! We have gay neighbors we are getting to know, and we know the "What does your faith/God say about us?" question is coming. If all this isn't difficult enough, we also have to navigate our way through the horrible conflict going on in the church.

The tragic thing about this battle is that it's being played out very publicly, and to be honest, it's pretty ugly. All this has contributed to a larger reality that now needs to be factored in, one that has both missional and generational impact.

MISSING A GENERATION

In 2009 the Barna Research Group published the book *unChristian*. The title itself represents the findings of the research. Unchurched people ages sixteen to thirty-five were asked what they thought of Christians. The overwhelming majority said they found Christians to be "un-Christian"! Strange concept! And when it came to the reasons why people thought us un-Christian, the one on the very top of the list was our antigay sentiment.

Think about this for a minute. The most common thing any non-churched person in this age group thinks about Christians is that we are antigay! How did this happen? How did our very reputation as *Christlike* ones somehow get tied in to what we think about and how we treat gay people? The sad thing is that while we've been arguing theology, a new fashioning of our public identity has been taking place. My best guess as to how and why this happened is tied in with Jesus' warnings to us in both Luke and Matthew about judgment. Both texts find Jesus warning us not to judge. But in Luke's passage we also see the consequences of what happens when we *do* judge, "Do not judge, and you will not be judged. Do not condemn, and you will not be condemned. Forgive, and you will be forgiven. . . . *For with the measure you use, it will be measured to you*" (Luke 6:37-38, italics added).

I believe our judgmentalism has come back to bite us on the backside. We have judged and held an already marginal community at arm's length—and now we are reaping the consequences. Southern Baptist missiologist Ed Stetzer notes that based on the church's treatment of gay people alone, there will be more and more people unwilling to give Christians or churches a hearing.[1] This means that unless we fundamentally change the way we *relate* to the gay community, we run the risk of alienating not only the gay community but the larger cultural audience, all on our inability to love. This surely must put all our fighting into perspective. The way we have and are going about this can rightly be called a false witness to the gospel. Theology and witness are surely tied together.

The growing generational gap is being felt both outside and *inside* the church, again related to how Christians treat gay people.[2] This was highlighted again for me when we first moved to California. The debate over Proposition 8 (gay marriage) was in full swing.[3] Prop 8 said no. So if you were *for* gay marriages you had to vote no against Prop 8. If you were *against* gay marriage then you had to vote yes, affirming Prop 8.

I found it all a little confusing and wasn't sure whether a yes or a no vote was affirming or against. That was until I took a drive to the local market. In the distance I could see people waving giant "YES to Prop 8" placards. As I got closer I immediately knew they were against gay marriage. Why? Because they were a predominantly middle-aged, conservative-looking group—they looked like Christians! The only thing that confused me was that they were holding "YES" signs, and I'm used to Christians holding "NO" signs. Then, as I drove further along, I saw a whole bunch of younger, hip-looking people holding "NO to Hate; NO to Prop 8" placards. It was finally clear to me now what yes and no meant.

A few weeks later I was speaking at a women's group when a distraught mother approached me. She told me that her daughter was placarding down on the corner with her friends *against* Prop 8—that is, her daughter had a "NO" placard, protesting *for* gay marriage. The woman was genuinely angry and perplexed. How could her daughter do this? "She should know better," she declared. "After all—we're Christians!"

This story demonstrates a similar problem. These young Christians are part of the *same* (unchurched) generation that have judged the church for being un-Christian and antigay. They are the ones who have gay friends at their colleges and places of work. They are the ones *relationally* involved, dealing with the hard questions of "did God really say?" This generation is on the missional edge in a way their folks are not. Part of the problem is that the theology handed down (from their parents or churches) hasn't necessarily been able to assist them in their contexts. And who wants to be associated with a group of people who placard against their friends? Our younger people are being forced to choose between what appears to be a bad-tempered church (which their parents represent) and their LGBT friends.

Let's face it, many people in the church have formulated their theology in the abstract, divorced from any real relationship and without much knowledge of the nature and dynamics of homosexuality. How many evangelicals have meaningful contact with gay people? And most evangelical churches seem to take a harsh political stand. So when young people go looking for answers, they don't expect to find them in the authority of parents or ecclesial institutions. Nor have they seen how a traditional/orthodox position on this issue has worked its way out missionally and relationally.

This is one of the reasons why I'm finding more and more younger Christians embracing a gay-affirming theology. It's not necessarily because they are convinced about the biblical arguments and exegesis (although for some it is), but because it *feels* like a more loving response. For many in the younger generation it's not necessarily as much about correct *doctrine* as it is about correct *loving*. The traditionalist side seems harsh, judgmental and bigoted. We have baptized whole categories of sin like greed and pride, only to pick on an apparently already-marginalized people. It just looks bad.

So, this turns out to be a fraught and complex issue indeed—it's much more than simply about crossing your theological t's and dotting your theological i's; it has a lot to do with the nature of our witness in our various contexts. I have often wondered just how big this debate would have been if we had been loving the LGBT community well all along. With all this in mind, it's time to look (albeit briefly) at the two dominant views regarding the validity of gay relationships from a Christian perspective.

> How it must have shocked the religious establishment of his day to hear Jesus proclaim that the prostitutes and tax collectors would enter the kingdom of God before the Pharisees.
>
> Greg Boyd,
> *Repenting of Religion*[4]

TWO UGLY STEPSISTERS!

With a cursory reading of the two views one might be inclined to think that when all is said and done it boils down to whether you think the Scriptures are *for* or *against* gay relationships, or more specifically whether you believe gay sexual relations are or are not appropriate for followers of Jesus. But in reality it's much more complicated than that. The reasons range from biblical authority, hermeneutics, what is considered normal and abnormal, inherited views from broader culture, political leanings, and so on (as well as the broader generational shifts I have already mentioned). And given the limitations of this chapter (and book) I can only give you a very quick (ridiculously so) overview of them.

The theological debate is essentially around four things:

1. Whether the relevant biblical texts about homosexuality are applicable today, given that we have learned much more about issues of sexual orientation and the like.

2. How does one interpret these relevant texts?

3. Do the creation narratives establish male-female relationships as normative and therefore the only sexual relationship endorsed by God?

4. What are God's priorities and purposes? Should Christians be more troubled about threats to the purity of the community and direct violations of biblical law codes, or is sin primarily understood as to how we mistreat the poor, the vulnerable and the marginalized? That is, should the church be focused on the moral aspects of the supposed misbehavior *of* homosexual people—or should the church be focused on the sin of the alleged misbehavior *toward* homosexual people?[5]

On one side we have the "traditionalists," on the other the "progressives"—terrible categories that don't do justice to the vast array of difference within the two. I know many *traditional* progressives and *progressive* traditionalists! Suggesting people are simply one or the other based on what they think about homosexuality seems weird to me. But whatever one does think on the issue, you *will* fall somewhere on the spectrum between the two. Even those still "making up their minds" are sitting with their old opinion (no matter how loosely), while they entertain the new.

Traditionalists generally lean toward saying that most if not all the biblical texts mentioning homosexuality are valid and normative, and therefore are applicable today. The progressives tend to say that they are obscure and culturally located texts that are not binding. The traditionalists affirm that the Bible explicitly forbids homosexual sex; the progressives say that the teachings of the Bible do not address our modern-day understanding of homosexuality and can therefore be bypassed. Regarding creational intent, the conservatives make a claim for exclusive male-female relationships and argue that life itself (the possibility of reproduction) requires this view. The progressives don't believe that heterosexual relationships provide the standard for all relationships. The progressive tends to see that the church's prime sin is in its unloving actions and attitudes toward gay people; the conservative thinks the primary sin as existing in homosexual behavior itself.

Point 4 on the list seems to be a point of tension for many who hold a more traditional view on the other points. Many see the failure to love and serve (as part of the church's witness in the world), and the belligerence associated with hateful actions, as more damaging to God's purposes than what some individuals choose to do in bed. And many have abandoned the traditionalist approach for exactly these reasons. They want to be people of love and grace, and see no viable, living alternative than to adopt the progressive view. Yet surely we can hold an orthodox position and still be good, kind and embracing people. That certainly is the challenge for those, like me, whose conscience holds them to a more traditional understanding.

AN ANATOMY OF DISCERNMENT

Two helpful guidelines I have drawn upon in wrestling through some of the theological stuff are the Wesleyan Quadrilateral and the "redemptive-movement hermeneutic" proposed by New Testament professor William J. Webb. Let me briefly describe each.

The Whatrilateral? The Wesleyan Quadrilateral is a helpful guide for arriving at faithful theological conclusions, and an extremely useful tool for helping us with sexual ethics.

There are four dimensions that together inform one's discernment: *Scripture, tradition, experience* and *reason*.[6] In chapter four, "The Eight *Fun*damentals of Sex," I noted how prone our sexuality is to being deceived. This is due, in part, to the overwhelming feelings that come along with our *experience* of sexuality, making it hard to be objective and make correct rational choices. The quadrilateral as a tool of discernment gives credence to how we might *feel* but provides us with three other pillars to help bring a more balanced approach to our discernment. Incorporating *Scripture* (as one's primary source), *reason* (recognizing God has created us as rational beings able to comprehend and discover God's truth), *tra-*

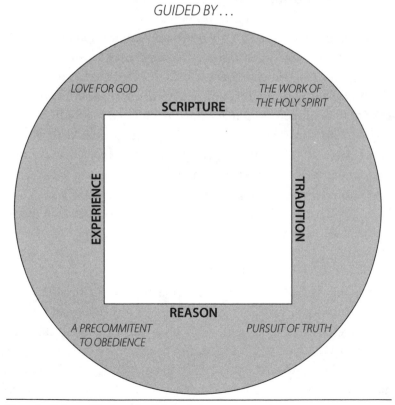

Figure 8.1. Enhanced Wesleyan Quadrilateral.

dition (drawing on wisdom of the people of God, both past and present) along with *experience* (how we *feel*) helps us minimalize the potential for being led astray or seeing emotions alone as the final authority.

The work and guidance of the Holy Spirit is also crucial. The Spirit first inspired the writing of the Scriptures and continues to inspire and guide us as we seek to interpret them, our history and personal experience. The Spirit brings us into the knowledge of God.

In figure 8.1 I have enhanced the four components of the quadrilateral with a commitment to the leading of the Holy Spirit, approaching Scripture along with a *precommitment to obey it* and guided by our primary commitment to *love for God*, which is a necessary guard against idolatry and deception.

The quadrilateral's balanced approach validates our human *experience*—how we *feel*—but also protects it within the boundaries of *Scripture, tradition* and *reason*. When these are governed by love for God, pursuit of truth and a precommitment to obedience, no matter what the outcome, we have a powerful combination to guide us in determining God's truth and will for us.[7]

Upward, onward. What I love about William Webb's redemptive forward movement is that while it is wonderfully complex for those who like that sort of stuff, for others, like me, he quickly makes sense of what could potentially end up being pretty dense material.[8]

Webb presents a type of X-Y-Z movement. X represents the original culture, Y represents the biblical text, and Z represents the "ultimate ethic" toward which the commands and principles of Scripture are pointing.[9] One must first assess the original culture in which the Scriptures were written and then study the biblical texts (first Old and then New Testaments) that relate to the ethical issue being addressed, and then formulate a position based on the movement in the idea or teaching over time. By seeing the movement of redemptive intention we can sense both the trajectory as well as something of the inner logic of the gospel. By discerning the intra-

canonical trajectory of certain ideas or teachings, we can determine
their validity over us today (see fig. 8.2).[10]

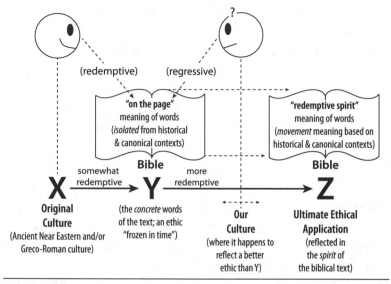

Figure 8.2. Webb's redemptive-movement hermeneutic.

Having suggested this as a way of discerning God's will in the
Word, Webb then compares the issues of slavery and the status and
treatment of women with that of homosexuality. Exploring the
teachings of the Old Testament and then discerning the develop-
ments in thinking in the New Testament, he suggests that there is
a clear forward "redemptive movement" with both women and
slaves. In other words, the logic of the gospel is clearly against
racism, slavery and oppression of women. But sadly, the self-same
biblical logic cannot be identified when it comes to the issue of
homosexuality. Every Scripture that mentions homosexual behavior, however understood, is clearly seen in the negative. There
are no affirming Scriptures and, more important for Webb, no
forward redemptive movement at all. Even in a culture that had
relative acceptance, God's Word was clear in its direction. While
Paul (in theory) could have easily exhorted gay people to restrict

themselves to monogamous relationships (which would suggest a redemptive forward movement), he doesn't. In fact he seems to completely rule out any homosexual activity as behavior outside of God's ethical boundary. In figure 8.3, Webb includes (W) to represent our culture.[11]

[W] →	X →	Y →	Z
our culture	**original culture**	**Bible**	**ultimate ethic**
almost complete acceptance and no restriction of homosexual activity	mixed acceptance and no restrictions of homosexual activity	negative assessment and complete restriction of homosexual activity	negative assessment and complete restriction of homosexual activity and greater understanding and compassion

Figure 8.3. The world and the redemptive-movement hermeneutic.

Let's take a closer look at the issue of slavery. What Paul writes in the New Testament about slavery can seem (from where we stand today) a little behind the times (see regressive image in fig. 8.2), but when we look at the context in which he was writing we see that he is actually quite radical. His new and kingdom-minded approach toward slaves would have seemed somewhat shocking to those reading his letters. Paul is trying to push the church to move closer toward the ultimate ethic (Z). We see this same redemptive forward movement between Israel and other societies. Even though slavery was an acceptable part of the Old Testament culture, Israel's slaves were given significantly more "rights" than they were elsewhere.

From the Old Testament to the New, we can easily observe a more significant liberalizing bias in regard to slavery at work. For one, the Messiah even dignifies and redeems the slave in taking on the same status in his incarnation (Philippians 2:7; John 13:1-17 [Jesus washing feet]). Because of Jesus' person and work, the gospel radically changes the equation of how we relate to each other—and this includes the interrelation of the master and slave. Once again we observe forward redemptive movement. So eventually when slavery as a system was declared sinful and wrong, the church *finally* came to the correct, absolutely *biblical* conclusion—albeit seventeen centuries later! No one today could or would make a theological case for slavery!

Whatever ethical issue we might face (see fig. 8.4) we are called to carefully read all relevant Scriptures and give particular attention to the inner movement within the canon itself. Do we sense in the biblical teachings a critical response to the surrounding cultural practices? Do they move toward a redemptive stance or is the issue at hand always prohibited? Once a trajectory or progression can be discerned, we can develop something of what Webb calls an "ultimate ethic" and live from that.

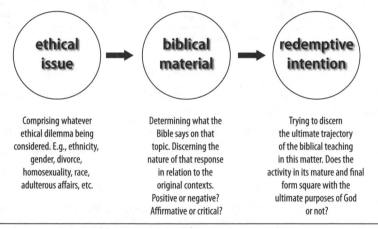

ethical issue	biblical material	redemptive intention
Comprising whatever ethical dilemma being considered. E.g., ethnicity, gender, divorce, homosexuality, race, adulterous affairs, etc.	Determining what the Bible says on that topic. Discerning the nature of that response in relation to the original contexts. Positive or negative? Affirmative or critical?	Trying to discern the ultimate trajectory of the biblical teaching in this matter. Does the activity in its mature and final form square with the ultimate purposes of God or not?

Figure 8.4. Redemptive movement in the Scriptures.

Webb is careful to note that while we can't discern a forward redemptive movement in Scripture regarding homosexual behavior, we must on every other level affirm the humanity and dignity of LGBT people, and work toward redemptive relationships as we engage them:

> Of equal importance, however, is the need to live redemptively in our relationships with gay men and lesbian women. Creating a redemptive focus to our lives means that we love homosexual people as ourselves. It means that we treat them with the same

kind of grace, respect, care and compassion with which we want to be treated. It means that we fight alongside of them against hateful action aimed at their community. It means all of the above, even if we do not agree with their sexual ethic.[12]

LEAD WITH EMBRACE

When it comes to these sorts of issues I find that Christians on the traditional side of things tend to lead (relationally speaking) with their theological position, often making it hard to embrace the person. Remember the old slogan "Love the sinner, hate the sin"? The problem is that very few in the church ever got around to loving the sinner—it became a cheap slogan. We must lead with our embrace, not our theology. When we lead with our theology, we tend to get all caught up in the "wrongness" of some people's behavior, and the humanness of the person is easily lost.

I have shared this "lead with embrace, not theology" principle countless times, and I inevitably get someone in my audience who can't quite get their mind around it, thinking that embracing someone equates to condoning their lifestyle choices. Yet passages like Romans 5:8, "While we were still sinners, Christ died for us," provide for us Christ's example. Jesus didn't wait for us to get our behaviors cleaned up *before* he embraced us; he embraced us first, with open arms. Working this out relationally with people is always a little more complex, but it is essential with our gay friends and family members that we don't close the relational doors. As one of my friends reminds me, embrace *is* theology.

This is, in my humble opinion, one of the biggest issues facing those on the traditional side of the debate. Many people have formulated their theological position devoid of any real contact (or understanding) of the very people it has been formulated about. But this is not how theology is supposed to work. It should be worked out in the robustness of human relationships, with all the love, pain and angst that accompanies them. Radical engagement and loving of the other earns us the right to speak. Yet many continue to enter the debate without even knowing a gay person. We need to *feel* this issue, not just *think* it.

==========

Love the sinner,
hate your own sin.

Tony Campolo

==========

Or in the words of Walter Brueggemann, "theology that is 'pre-pain' must be treated with suspicion."[13] In other words, let our theology get under our skin, think about how it must *feel* for those about whom we are developing it. It really isn't enough to have a "correct" theology anymore (as if it ever was); it's about getting the sincere, relational love stuff together.

Let me end this chapter with a missional story of how we can lead with embrace and help people take redemptive steps forward toward the ideals of the kingdom—even if they are not yet believers![14]

Stuart and Ben both worked as prostitutes on a street corner near where I lived. I had grown to love and respect these guys, not because they were living a lifestyle in line with the kingdom (how can selling your body to desperate old men be that?) but because they had a resilience, a strength about them, evidenced in many ways, including their open-hearted generosity, hospitality and warmth—despite their desperate circumstance.

They invited me over one day because they had hit an impasse in their relationship. As I arrived I quickly found myself embroiled in the midst of a very messy argument. I went into counseling mode and found myself giving them basic relational tools to help them get through their gridlock. It was a complex situation, but I felt by the time I left they were in a much better place.

On the way home I had a weird little realization. Many Christians, thinking I should really be telling them how bad their lifestyles are (like they haven't heard that before!), would probably judge me for helping Stuart and Ben get over their relationship problems. I was teaching them to listen, to be kind, to forgive, all kingdom values. I wasn't teaching them to have better sex.

Opening people up to redemptive *forward* principles will help them move closer to God way more than by telling them how far they fall short. Engaging with people *wherever* they find themselves or we find them, and then slowly and intentionally pointing them toward the ideals of the kingdom and therefore God, is wonderfully liberating.

Each and every one of us, and on every level, ought to be moving closer toward the ideals of God. That's what happens when we partner with the Holy Spirit and experience the inner work of renewal within us. Each of us, wherever we are at in our discipleship, no matter what the issue, with the help of the Holy Spirit continues to step into greater kingdom living—that's what it is to bring a little of heaven to earth.

Part Three

THE MISSION OF
CHRISTIAN SEXUALITY

9

The Bent Scapegoat

Homosexuality is the scare issue in the churches. It has become a funnel into which is poured a whole range of social fears, many of which have little, if any, relation to issues of sexual orientation.

JAMES B. NELSON AND SANDRA P. LONGFELLOW

We must all realize that prejudice and resentment come more easily to man than insight and appreciation. Love is health, and truth is the only serum: yet truth is a product of learning, and love is scarce.

ABRAHAM HESCHEL

One of the most powerful confessions I've ever heard was from a pastor who attended one of my workshops. He talked about a young man who came to his office to talk. The pastor welcomed him, and after they shook hands they took their seats and began to talk casually. Eventually, after some prodding, the guy reluctantly revealed his reason for meeting. He told the pastor that he was gay and didn't know what to do. The pastor said that after hearing this he just couldn't concentrate and eventually excused himself to go to the bathroom. At this point he paused and said to me, "I don't know what happened then. I know it was irrational, and I'm deeply embarrassed telling you, but once in the bathroom I experienced an overwhelming need to wash my hands." He said he had no clue why he did it; he just felt an urgent need to cleanse himself of this guy's handshake.

Now this pastor wasn't proud of what he did, but this also wasn't the end of the story. God began convicting him of his actions and challenged him to pray for this young man, which he did. He also felt he was meant to keep meeting with him, so he offered this to the young man, which he accepted. Over the weeks as this young man's story continued to unfold, the pastor's heart was changed. He proudly stated to me toward the end of our conversation, "I never needed to wash my hands again. In fact, I hug him regularly now!" God was at work in their relationship, not just for the young man but for the pastor.

UNCLEAN HANDS

Richard Beck, in his deeply insightful book *Unclean: Meditations on Purity, Hospitality, and Mortality*, helps us understand what is going on here. He talks about a phenomenon called "disgust and contamination psychology."[1] Disgust is one of those deeply ingrained, universal human expressions; we all feel it, and with a variety of things. And usually along with this is an irrational sense of contamination; we think that what disgusts us can also contaminate us.

Think about the feeling we get when we discover a hair in our soup. Our first response is to screw up our nose. We feel a sense of disgust. What follows closely behind is a feeling of dis-ease with continuing to eat the soup, even after the hair has been removed. That's because we now feel that the whole bowl of soup has become contaminated.[2]

Beck's book is a stimulating read, but his prime interest lies in how disgust psychology plays itself out in the life of the church, specifically as it relates to purity codes. In bringing psychology to play with theology he looks at themes presented in Matthew 9, where Jesus attends a party at Matthew's house. "While Jesus was having dinner at Matthew's house, many tax collectors and sinners came and ate with him and his disciples. When the Pharisees saw this, they asked his disciples, 'Why does your teacher eat with tax collectors and sinners?'" (vv. 10-11). The Pharisees are outraged that Jesus is hanging out with undesirables, so they challenge him. Jesus responds, "It is not the healthy who need a doctor, but the sick. But go and learn what this means: '*I desire mercy, not sacrifice.*' For I have not come to call the righteous, but sinners" (vv. 12-13, italics added).

In this context Beck sees *mercy* and *sacrifice* as two impulses that pull in opposite directions and are inherently incompatible. Sacrifice (in the ancient sense) by its very nature draws boundaries, distinguishing categories of clean and unclean. It is required for the purification of an individual or community. Mercy, on the other hand, knows no boundaries. It is inherently hospitable and open. Beck observes, "Sacrifice—the purity impulse—marks off a zone of holiness, admitting the 'clean' and expelling the 'unclean.' Mercy, by contrast, crosses those purity boundaries. Mercy blurs the distinction, bringing clean and unclean into contact. Thus the tension."[3]

Think of this in the context of the church. The logic of disgust psychology is that we manifest disgust or repulsion toward those who have violated what we perceive as the purity codes, usually connected to the body and especially to do with sexuality. Boundaries are drawn, in effect separating ourselves because we are afraid if we get too close we risk being polluted by them, just like the Pharisees in Matthew 9. Closeness evokes a disgust response (screwing up of the nose) and any touch gives one a feeling like he or she has been contaminated—like the handshake with the pastor (or the hair in the soup).

I can't tell you how many people confess to me these kinds of feelings. And let's be honest, once we get to this place where a sense of contagion sets in, it's very hard to reverse it. Beck explains,

Once an object is deemed to be contaminated there is very little that can be done to rehabilitate the object. . . . Pastorally speaking, this may be why sexual sins, which are uniquely structured by the purity metaphor in many churches, elicit more shame and guilt. In short, although a church might claim that all sins are "equal" (in their offensiveness to God), sins have different psychological experiences.[4]

Think on this and the sins that make you feel uncomfortable. While we are told scripturally that all sins are the same, we still *feel* like some are worse. This is exactly what Beck is talking about. "Sins might indeed be equal, theologically speaking, but the *experience* of a given sin can be very, very different depending upon the psychology regulating the experience."[5] It's not just about what we *know*, cognitively speaking (i.e., all sins are the same), it's how we *feel*, viscerally speaking, which in my experience is often the more powerful of the two.

Let me give you another example.

DISCIPLING NOSES AND HOLY ENGAGEMENT

I often challenge people who give to the poor or homeless (usually from a very safe distance) to take a further step toward them; in other words, get up close and personal. Now most people find that difficult for a variety of reasons. But one common reason is because some homeless people stink! Their smell separates us. Yet the message of the gospel propels us toward connection, so if our noses are restricting us from engagement, then we need to disciple them! If we don't train our bodies to get beyond our psychological and visceral responses, we will never move beyond those we feel comfortable with.

Now, all this might sound a little heavy, and it is. But we really need to be careful with this stuff. We follow a Jesus who broke down barriers between the clean and unclean, and gave access to people that offended the purity sensibilities of the religious. He bridged the gap between the *us* and *them*. Jesus modeled a different type of purity—a holiness of engagement, not exclusion.

A question we must ask is, What was it about the holiness of Jesus that drew people to him like a magnet? Sinners of all sorts were drawn into his orbit: the bungled, the broken and the bent, tax collectors, harlots—all sorts of social outcasts—all wanting closeness. His holiness was certainly alluring and enticing. Following this, a more disturbing question needs to be asked: What is it about more churchy forms of holiness that seems to evoke the opposite response? Sinners seem to be repelled by Christians! They certainly are not rushing forward to hang out with us. I want to suggest that perhaps this is not holiness at all but a counterfeit form of moralism.

The Gospels clearly show us that social rejects loved to be around Jesus. Think of prostitutes, lepers, tax collectors, adulterers, Roman mercenaries, Samaritans, Gentiles, and the list goes on. There was something compelling about his brand of holiness;

> After coming into contact with a religious man I always feel I must wash my hands.
>
> Friedrich Nietzsche

people couldn't get enough of him. By hanging out with people like these, Jesus shows us that one cannot achieve holiness by separation from the unclean. As previously mentioned, our community at "South" became something of a refuge for similar types of people— prostitutes, schizophrenics and the like—and I know from personal experience that they *don't generally like Christians*. How can they love Jesus and so dislike his followers? Surely if we were more Christlike they would want to be around us as well.

The even more amazing thing is that not only did the social outcasts and sinners want to be around Jesus, but Jesus wanted to be around them! This was the whole purpose of Jesus' mission, to save "sinners" (Luke 19:10), and he practiced active *proximity* with them. Jesus the Holy One often went out of his way to connect with, or be seen with, those who the "holy ones" of the day would have never thought of entertaining. The holiness of Jesus, it seems, is a redemptive, *missional*, world-embracing holiness that does not separate itself from the world, but rather liberates it.

SUSAN'S STORY

Let me tell you another story that is a little more common; it's about my friend's friend Susan. Susan's story is nothing new or startling, but in the five minutes it took for her to blurt it out to me she touched on almost every concern or faulty perception that Christians have when it comes to homosexuality or gay people.

Her story was about one of the families in her street. She went to lengths to paint a perfect picture of them. Using terms like *attractive, active in the community, really nice people, liked by everybody, great parents* and a more than regular use of the word *normal*. She was building a picture of the super-suburban family. Then it all fell apart . . .

The couple announced they were getting divorced. The wife had declared herself to be a lesbian and was leaving her husband for her "special" friend. This special friend was described by Susan as pretty "butch" looking, as opposed to her neighbor who was very "normal" looking. "But I'd suspected something was up for a while," reported Susan, "My neighbor's from Berkeley; I should have known."

She continued, "They know we're Christians, so they know where we stand, but how can I still talk to her? Won't she think I'm condoning what she's doing? And what about my kids? How do I shelter and protect them?" Susan was genuinely distressed. This was no gossip session; she wanted to help. This was a situation she hadn't encountered before, and she honestly didn't know what to do.

In these moments I have to take a deep breath—not in a rolling of the eyes kind of way but because I know that what I'm dealing with here is not just surface concerns. There are usually much deeper issues at work, and they are not always easy to confront.

WHAT LIES BENEATH

What exactly is it about homosexuality that seems to send people into a tailspin? I doubt Susan would have had the same degree of anxiety if her neighbor was leaving her husband for another man. Nor would she have felt quite the same need to protect her kids. She may still have asked for my advice, but I'm sure she would have felt more confident with the whole situation.

All of us have little fears and anxieties that lurk beneath the surface—fears of people who are different from us, those we deem the *other*. And these fears, if not dealt with, begin to foster negative thoughts and prejudices. Sometimes we don't even become aware of our prejudices until they are standing in front of us! One of the problems with fear and prejudice is that it creates social distance, which only reinforces the fear. And when social distance is violated, discrimination can result. In other words, as long as the feared *other* doesn't interfere with me and mine, they are tolerated (at best). At worst, they are treated with hostility and even violence.

> There is no prejudice so strong as that which arises from a fancied exemption from all prejudice.
>
> **William Hazlitt**

We ought never underestimate what a little fear and prejudice can do. I have seen some pretty cruel and irrational behavior dished out by Christians. And while most people like Susan really do want to learn and love, her language and response indicate some underlying issues that first need to be addressed. For Susan and many of us, gay people represent the stranger, the *other*. We see them as not quite normal. And unless we take steps to make the unknown *known*, we risk letting fear, not love, dictate the terms of the relationship.

Fear of gay people doesn't just arise because we don't know or understand them, it also comes from the harmful attitudes we have absorbed from centuries of negativity and discrimination. Historically speaking, gay people have rarely been given a good rap. In fact quite the opposite: they have been stigmatized, set apart for ridicule and prejudice, often beaten up, sometimes involving serious crimes. It's only really been in the last few decades, along with our increased understanding of homosexuality, that societal attitudes have begun changing. The only tragedy about this is that it hasn't been the church leading the way!

WE AND THEY

Fuller Seminary president and author Mark Labberton, in his brilliant book *The Dangerous Act of Loving Your Neighbor*, says all of us experience a fundamental alienation toward the *other*. It's important that we recognize that this takes place within our own hearts.

> The ways of the heart are reflected in the world daily in how we perceive (see and assess one another), how we name (frame and position one another) and how we act (engage or distance one another). These three are inseparable, simultaneous but distinguishable, and they are a potent force.[6]

Labberton is absolutely right. And much of this assessment and positioning takes place without us even stopping to think about it. And if how we act toward a person (either engage or distance ourselves) comes from faulty or inaccurate assessments, then it's no wonder we keep at a safe distance.

Labberton goes on to talk about the categories of "we" and "they" that we all operate from. *We* being the collective "I"—people we know, understand, who have similar perspectives on life, a shared value system and so on—those we feel safe with. *They* being the "others." He explains something of the attitude these categories form within us.

> Saying *we* is like building a kind of perch for ourselves. *We* functions, then, as a kind of social place from which we see, act, engage or withdraw from them and that. It's a powerful

perch that motivates so much about how we perceive, name and understand ourselves in the world. . . .

They as a word involves figuratively sticking out your tongue. It's a word of expulsion. *They* is a word that pushes away. It's not far from spitting. It draws a boundary, a perimeter, a distinction, a separation, a distance. *They* is a kind of anti-identity, an anti-definition of *I* or *we*.[7]

These words are both powerful and confronting, and raise the question of who represents the *we* and the *they* for us, and what assumptions and attitudes we hold toward those we categorize as *they*.

Susan's neighbor moved from being a *we* to a *they*, and in the process became captive to Susan's preformed attitudes about gay people. Her status (as well as her posture) changed—everything about her now subsumed under the label "gay." Whereas she was once normal and safe, now Susan's neighbor was someone the children needed to be protected from.

> It is harder to crack a prejudice than an atom.
>
> **Albert Einstein**

It's been said that this positive valence of *we* (or *us*, i.e., *heterosexuals*) and the negative valence of *they* (or *them*, i.e., *homosexuals*) has been the basis for stigmatizing the homosexual person. *They* are different, not quite normal, therefore to be feared, even hated, certainly pitied and devalued.[8] The same prejudice of course has been leveled at other communities on the margins, groups like Jews, blacks and foreigners.

I have seen this play out many times. Parents rejecting sons and daughters, pastors dispelling congregants, friends abandoning friends, all because they found out they were gay. Individuals once known and loved become a *they*. It's like being gay fundamentally changes everything else about a person. It's no wonder some hide that part of themselves. The relational risk and potential judgment is too great.

WHO IS NORMAL?

This brings us to the issue of what constitutes normal. As Susan's story unfolded there was an (unconscious) assessment taking place of what she perceived was and wasn't "normal." Her more than average use of the word was evidence of this. Clearly what happened for her was outside of those bounds. Homosexuality—the "abnormal"—had now shattered her sense of what is "normal." The truth is that we all do this. In fact every living culture and society creates standards and boundaries around what is and isn't normal: this helps make some sense of the world, while creating standards and order.[9]

And let's be honest here, homosexuality *isn't* the norm—that's a fact. Heterosexuality (by sheer numbers) is the norm.[10] And this isn't necessarily the problem. The problem arises when the deviation (to the norm) becomes depersonalized and attributed to being less than human or morally deficient. This is exactly what has happened to gay people; they have been seen as less than others, *ab*-normal, therefore to be feared, stigmatized and discriminated against. This is why there have been such strong moves within broader society to normalize being gay. While there has been a significant shift in this direction, we still have a long way to go.

I believe that the church needs to get behind this normalization process—despite what one thinks theologically. Homosexual people are in the end just people. Their story and their struggles are essentially no different from yours and mine. They, like all bearers of God's image, are worthy of dignity and respect. So what I mean by normalization here is simply the recognition that homosexuality is part of the spectrum of human sexuality. It's one of the ways sexuality expresses itself in and throughout ordinary human experience and history. It might be less frequent, but it is undeniably present as an expression throughout. The fact is that homosexuality *is* being normalized throughout Western culture as I write. Legislation is now being systematically rolled out across the United States (and most of the Western world, for that matter) that recognizes the full citizenship and human rights of homosexual people. There is simply no going back. This "normalizing" of homosexuality needs to be accepted and responded to in Christlike ways.

This is not just an issue about our witness to and treatment of those outside the community of faith but for those with same-sex attraction within the church. Until this issue is on the table we are never going to get rid of the taboo and stigma, and really get to encounter these people for whom Christ died. We will continue to make it very hard for people within the church (who are gay) to feel normal.

Recently a young man revealed to me his inner struggle with homosexuality. It took him such a long time to get there that I was expecting something completely different. My initial response was to laugh and say, "Is that all! I thought you were going to confess to being a mass murderer or something!" He later shared with me that my laughing was deeply healing for him. It helped dispel some of the power the stigma of homosexuality held over him. This is what I mean by normalizing.

THE NORMALITY OF DREAD

My sister wasn't "normal," because she had one leg. And as much as my parents tried to treat her as they did everyone else, at school she was quickly singled out. I spent many of our early school years getting into fights on her behalf, all because she didn't look normal. School-yards can be cruel places where our differences and stigmas are brutally defined and then in turn define us. Bullying is a real problem with tragic consequences in and out of school. We all know the reality of this. Some of us have kids who don't fit in. Some of us *were* those kids.

It might be easy to forgive this type of dehumanizing in the schoolyard, for kids are kids, after all. But the problem is that bullying transcends the playground and works its way through whole societies and marks whole generations, with devastating consequence. Nazi Germany is just one, admittedly rather extreme, case in point. In this context my sister (and other differently abled people) would have been exterminated alongside Jews, homosexuals, Gypsies and other *ab*normal people. In Hitler's system when one deviated from the true norm (as defined by him and the prejudices of history), one ceased to be considered human. When the perceived humanity of a person is lost, their life fails to have any intrinsic worth in the eyes of others. As sociologist Erving Goffman says, "By definition, of course, we believe the person with a stigma is not quite human."[11] Think about this for a moment.

Now, we may not be living in Hitler's Germany, but people still die because of their stigmas, some by the hands of others, and tragically some at their own hands.[12] As crazy as it seems, sometimes those with the very same stigmas can become the greatest threat. Some of the most horrific acts of homophobic abuse have been at the hands of those who experience a form of "homosexual dread"— a fear of their own latent homosexuality. This is the only way one can understand fallen pastor Ted Haggard's homophobic vitriol, only to be found himself having a homosexual encounter.

A friend of mine struggled with this in his early years before he officially "came out." He used to hang around with a gang who would go out in search of gay guys and assault them. He would then sneak back later to have sex with these same guys he had abused! He was living two very different (conflicted) lives. It's interesting that research confirms this type of conflicted behavior.

One such study was conducted on a group of men claiming to be heterosexual. Those in the study who professed more overt homophobic attitudes were actually found to be more aroused by homosexual images.[13] Another study showed similar links, highlighting how many homophobic people were "at war" with themselves and prone to "turning the internal conflict outward," pointing to figures such as Haggard.[14] Targeting a known or suspected homosexual for ridicule or abuse, the abuser in effect (psychologically and socially speaking) distances him- or herself from them.

DON'T GET TOO CLOSE!

Even if homophobia doesn't result in physical harm, the stigma that exists still represents a kind of social death. In their stirring book *Is the Homosexual My Neighbor?* Letha Scanzoni and Virginia Mollenkott claim that

> most heterosexual people tend to think of homosexual people as so different and so far removed from the norm that it's almost as though they belong to a different species or come from another planet. Or, if human at all, homosexuals are considered so strange or depraved or sick, or sinful that "respectable" people will be sure to keep them at a distance.[15]

Going back to Susan's story, it's not too hard to make the jump from this to the need of protecting our kids. This was of great concern to Susan, and has been echoed in many debates over whether gay people should be in positions of influence over kids (e.g., as teachers or Sunday school leaders, etc.). All of this is based around the protection of one's children from some perceived threat or fear of homosexual people.

Now I understand the parental instinct is to protect children from harm. But if shielding our children from those who are different is based on irrational thinking and fear, then it can no longer be considered as being protective but rather as transmitting prejudice.

I AM WHAT YOU THINK!

Another way of looking at this whole issue is to see it through the lens of stereotypes. Stereotyping is the social narrative we use to maintain prejudice, and there is no question that homosexuality has been profoundly stereotyped.

Stereotyping is common and as old as human culture itself. Stereotypes themselves reflect ideas that we hold about those who are different from us. In many ways they are unavoidable because they help us categorize. And when used positively stereotypes help make our communication easier and nuance free. But the problem with stereotyping is twofold: first, not everyone (in a specific culture or people group) *fits* the given stereotype, and second, stereotyping easily leads to prejudice and discrimination.

Let's be honest, when it comes to gay and lesbian people, stereotypes abound! Given the degree of social distance between many people and the LGBT community, it's hard to break down the stereotypes that exist, or even have them challenged. Some people really do believe that all male homosexuals have limp wrists, speak with a lisp and are only interested in sex—and that all lesbians are butch looking and hate men!

Let's return to Susan. Out of her comfort zone and unable to make sense of what happened, she quickly resorted to stereotypes. How could a normal suburban mom end up running off with another woman? Well, it must have been because she went to a "liberal" university. And her neighbor's special friend is suddenly labeled "butch"—her appearance until this point might not have embodied quite the same meaning.

This type of stereotyping happens all of the time and often without much thought. Even if seemingly harmless among friends, we really need to be careful. An example occurred recently when a friend (who is discreet about his gay orientation) was asked by someone to reveal his homosexuality to a certain female so she would feel safe with him. (It's a complicated story.) The reason that was given was, "If she knows you're gay, she'll just think you're one of the girls." Now the comment wasn't meant to offend him, but it is certainly making a statement about his masculinity. He is not one of the girls, nor does he want to be. But because he is gay certain things are assumed.

But not all stereotyping is done thoughtlessly or without harmful intent. Gordon Allport, author and psychologist, says the difference between a harmless generalization and a real prejudice is about our ability to change our opinion.

If a person is capable of rectifying his erroneous judgments in the light of new evidence he is not prejudiced. *Prejudgments become prejudices only if they are not reversible when exposed to new knowledge.* A prejudice, unlike a simple misconception, is actively resistant to all evidence that would unseat it. We tend to grow emotional when a prejudice is threatened with contradiction. Thus the difference between ordinary prejudgments and prejudice is that one can discuss and rectify a prejudgment without emotional resistance.[16]

I come up against this type of emotional resistance regularly. And to be honest, unless people actually get to know gay people *personally* and invest in meaningful relationships, they will simply continue to perpetuate the stereotypes. The fact is LGBT people come from all walks of life and races, are involved in all sorts of vocations, merely want to live "normal" lives with their loved ones, and contribute to society in ways that are fulfilling to them—just like you and me. But instead they are held captive by who *we* think they are—their individuality and uniqueness swallowed up in the impersonal and distorted stereotype.[17]

THINK WELL OF ME

Dave was challenged at church to get to know the neighbors he knew the least. He said he inwardly groaned because he knew who that was. Two gay guys had moved in down the road, and he had been doing all he could to avoid them. He even changed the way he came home in order not to pass by their house. Dave wasn't proud of this; it was just the way it was. He held many negative assumptions about gay people and freely used stereotypes in relation to them. Now he knew God was on to him.

After a couple of weeks trying to plan his approach, he accidently ran into them at the local hardware store. Given that he thought all gay men were into cooking or hair dressing, it was the last place he expected to see them. But here they were in the timber section. Knowing this was his moment he awkwardly approached one of them who was looking at the wood. "Oh, what are you building?" he asked, trying to be friendly. The guy told him he was building a bed for his son. Dave had to push himself on, fearing what might come next. The guy continued on saying that he and his partner had recently adopted a little boy.

Dave wanted out of there, not believing what he just heard. But before Dave could escape the guy asked him if he had any kids. Dave replied that he did. "We should bring our boy over," he offered. Dave now realized he was in trouble—it was one thing to talk to a gay person, but this was a whole other path he didn't want to go down.

As feared, the guys did bring their little boy over, and while Dave remained somewhat guarded, he eventually found out more about this little kid. The child they had adopted had Down Syndrome. His mother had abandoned him and his biological father was unknown. As Dave's relationship with them grew, he was struck time and time again with the love he saw these gay men give to this child.

By the time I met Dave, they had all become great friends, and he and his wife had welcomed this family into their home and hearts. He confessed to me his prior fear, and said these guys had totally blown his stereotype apart. And he was convinced that if he had not intentionally stepped into a relationship with them, he most certainly would have continued in his judgment of gay people. I'll never forget when he said to me, "You know what? After I got to know them, I realized they were just normal blokes."

I end with this because it is a wonderful story about a man who was willing to step outside his comfort zone and encounter a God who was at work in the midst of the love shown by two men toward this abandoned little child. Dave had prejudged but was willing to look again at people who were the *other* to him, and that made all the difference.

Imago Gay

God is love, and the capacity to love is man's innermost participation in God. This capacity is never lost but needs only to be purified to be raised to God Himself. Thus love is not only a feeling; it is the godly in existence. Nor can one love God unless he loves his fellow man, for God is present in man as in all of His creation.

MAURICE FRIEDMAN

Loving God must involve loving our neighbor.
Or we are not loving God.

MARK LABBERTON

Jesus summarized the whole of the commandments into two: loving God, and loving our neighbor as ourselves. The frustrating thing about this is that it is both profoundly simple *and* difficult at the same time. And the difficulty seems to be especially apparent when our neighbor also happens to be gay.

Al and I recently co-purchased and moved into a home with a bunch of friends in Los Angeles. Like all moving days it was pretty chaotic, with people everywhere and boxes all over the place. I was trying to bring some order to the mess that was to be our dining room when I turned around to find a man standing there. "Hello," he said, "I saw the moving vans, thought I'd drop in and say hi. My name is Sam. My partner, David, and I have lived next door for twenty-five years. Anything you need to know about the neighborhood we can tell you."

A few days later we walked out our front door (which opens onto the road) to find two men walking by with their dogs. One of the dogs was a Boxer that looked exactly like our beloved dog, Ruby, who we'd left back in Australia. Naturally, this prompted conversation and pats (for the dogs), and before we knew it, they, along with their dogs, were inside our home congratulating us on our purchase and meeting some of our household. We soon discovered that these neighbors lived just one street over, in what one of them described as "the house with the red door."

Two gay couples within the first week of moving in. In some way I felt strangely comforted and knew that God had not only led us to the right house but to the right neighborhood.

YOU ARE MY NEIGHBOR?

I am frequently asked by sincere Christians how they can "reach out" and love their gay neighbors, friends and colleagues—as if there is some sort of trick or special way of doing it. It's like a person's sexual orientation automatically qualifies them for a special category all of their own and therefore some special type of love is required. Yet there is nothing fundamentally different between a gay and a straight person, certainly nothing that requires a different genre of love. There ought to be no essential difference in how we treat anyone (in the faith or without).

When we begin to categorize people and push them into the "different" box, we inevitably push them further away from the obligation of neighborliness all disciples of Jesus are called to show. Remember Jesus' take on the question "Who is my neighbor?" (Luke

10:25-37). Disciples are to understand themselves through the lens of the neighborliness exercised by the good Samaritan and *not* the religious folk in the parable. Those of us who have gay friends, family or the like already know that the homosexually oriented person *is* our neighbor—they always were—the rest of us just need to catch up.

> I think there's just one kind of folks. Folks.
>
> Harper Lee

Nonetheless we must admit that differences do remain; otherwise we wouldn't find it so hard, right? There are cultural disparities that we need to be aware of, so sensitivity does need to be cultivated. This is not dissimilar to learning to love someone from another culture, socioeconomic background, age, gender and the like. In order to communicate lovingly we need to appreciate this, or we risk our love not being received in the way we intended.

When it comes to our gay neighbors, it is important to acknowledge the existing history between the church and LGBT community, and the stance many in the church have adopted toward them. We would be naive to think that we get to start with a blank slate. It will come as no surprise that there is a lot of very bad history between these two communities, resulting in a great deal of alienation—so much so that when two individuals from either community seek to engage even in friendly neighborly dialogue, it can end up being clumsy at the very least.

In this chapter I hope to identify some of these barriers and suggest some practical steps to move forward to a place of real human engagement, because if we don't, we'll never learn to really love our neighbor, be they gay, straight or anything in between!

SEE GOD IN THEM

We spent a lot of time in chapter nine talking about the danger of stereotyping and prejudice. In the same vein, probably the greatest hindrance to us loving our gay neighbor lies with our own faulty preconceptions. All of us carry some preset notions or assumptions about the other. These assumptions and attitudes are usually a mixture of personal experience, broader cultural and societal attitudes, media and the like. They may be accurate or inaccurate, idealized or stereotyped, whatever, but to us they will always appear to be real. Like it or not, to most people, perception *is* reality. So unless we actually engage in some form of relationship with the people themselves, we will likely never have our assumptions and attitudes challenged.

When Jesus asks us to love our neighbor, he is asking us to put our preformed attitudes to the side, to suspend judgment so that we might simply encounter them as they present themselves to us. I am not suggesting that this is easy to do, but practice will make perfect. It's only in the context of relationship that we can love. And let's face it, authentic loving is never comfortable or easy.

One of the most useful ways (and a personal discipline) that I find helpful with *any* person we might engage with is to focus first and foremost on how God sees the person rather than on how I do. This can require a pretty radical paradigm shift.

Years ago I heard a pastor pose a question: What is the first thing we could say about any person in the world? The majority of the Christian audience responded with the script that people were first and foremost sinners in need of salvation. He explained that while that was indeed true—all have sinned and fallen short—there was a still more fundamental truth; namely, every person is created in the image of God. Everyone carries a little piece of God in them. This truth precedes and qualifies *all* other things (including their fallenness) we might say about them.

Now while this might seem obvious to you, for me at the time it came as a significant paradigm shift and profoundly impacted the way I viewed people, especially those who didn't yet know Jesus. I have always been involved with some pretty messy people, along with some who have done some pretty awful things. And it's not that hard to focus on their sins or messy lifestyles. We can easily affirm that they are sinners in need of redemption. But the pastor was suggesting that we should first and foremost see all people as image bearers of God and only then see them as fallen and in need of salvation, that this was the right theological order and priority. We must get the order right, and this is why.

View 1

1. Sinner (primary truth)

2. Imago Dei (secondary truth)

View 1 sees people as sinners first and foremost. They are people under judgment before a holy God and in need of God's redemption.

When we see people first and foremost as sinners, the central focus is placed on their state of sinfulness as well as their acts of sin. It's a natural next step to become fixated with what, in our minds, might be the morally offensive behavior. Our job becomes primarily about cleaning them up, getting them to repent from their sinful ways so they will then behave correctly. But this view tends to limit the gospel to a combination of sin management and behavior modification. While the gospel addresses morality, it also condemns religious moralism. The problem with such a limited gospel is that it clouds our vision: we never see people how God sees them and how God made them—as beings of inestimable worth.

When I am focused on what I consider to be someone's bad behavior, I am less inclined to want to engage him or her. The person's behavior stands in the way of any real relationship. I'm unable to see

> When I respect the image of God in others, I protect the image of God in me. When Jesus speaks of loving our neighbor, it isn't just for our neighbor's sake. If we don't love our neighbor, something happens to us.
>
> Rob Bell

God's image until *after* the individual has repented and stopped the "ungodly" behavior.

View 2

1. Imago Dei (primary truth)

2. Sinner (secondary truth)

View 2 sees people as first and foremost created in the image of God. This means all people have an innate Godlike beauty and dignity because they all in their own unique way reflect something of their Creator. Yes, in some individuals, the image is profoundly marred; it might even appear that sometimes it is marred to the point of extinction, but in actual fact it is always there by virtue of their *being human* (Genesis 1:27).

Putting the imago Dei first causes us to focus on the greater truths about any person. We move away from our preformed cultural assumptions, and from fixating on behaviors, to focusing on their innate potential to imitate their Creator. There is always the possibility of goodness and great beauty in all people. *Seeing* like this changes everything. Our role becomes to look for God in them, to call forth the image, to fan it into flame, to help them to both see and become like the One they reflect. We still see the sin, but it no longer dominates our perspective; it merely qualifies it. Yes, people are sinners (secondary truth), but they are first and foremost image bearers.

First things must surely come first. We were, after all, created in God's image before we all (collectively and individually) fell into sin. So from a theological perspective we are on solid ground (Genesis 1 comes before Genesis 3). And from a missiological perspective it really does change the way we engage with the other. I am less inclined to be fearful and less inclined to judge when I approach the other as a being reflecting God. It is simply a more graceful, loving way to engage a lost and broken humanity. The fact is that Jesus saw humanity as worthy before any of us changed our behaviors (Romans 5:8).

This must become a practiced response. For too long we have engaged people primarily on the basis of their sinfulness and sin. God is at work in all of humanity, not because all know God but because all in some way reflect God, whether or not they (or we) see it. What does this mean then for our gay neighbors? It means we need to see them as they are: *first and foremost* as image bearers of our God. And we might be surprised what we find, as Bonhoeffer cautions us: "I can never know beforehand how God's image should appear in others. That image always manifests a completely new and unique form that comes solely from God's free and sovereign creation."[1] As my dear friend Cath constantly reminds me, unless people really suspend their judgments they'll never truly engage the other. We simply must look beyond behaviors and lifestyle choices that may or may not be offensive to us. Focus on the imago Dei and discover how that is being expressed in their lives.

FIND GOD WITH THEM

I mentioned in the introduction how God had been on my case for a long time, yet I didn't realize it. Even in my own very misguided way I was pursuing him. The truth is that God is on *everyone's* case! No matter who you are, where you are or what you are doing, God is in pursuit of you. He is the unrelenting evangelist.

John Wesley called this reality "prevenient grace" (literally "grace that prepares" or grace that goes ahead of us, preparing the way), and he built his entire evangelistic ministry on it. He believed that God was always preparing the way for the preaching of the gospel, that God was *at work in every person, calling them to himself in and through Jesus Christ.* It is a wonderfully biblical doctrine. Think about it: we don't carry God with us into any situation. As Lord of creation and history God is on the scene long before you or I arrive.[2] Our role is simply to look, listen, see and discern God's prevening work—what he is already doing in people's lives—and join with him!

Every person on the planet has theophanies, religious experiences or encounters that take us beyond simply what is seen to an awareness of a deeper level of reality. It might be the sunset that takes away our breath, the awe experienced at the birth of a child, the raw beauty of the ocean or the look in a lover's eyes. Sometimes they come via a conversation, where one experiences a revelation and dawning of a significant truth, or moments when time stands still and eternity fills the moment, what poet Gerard Manley Hopkins called an "inscape."[3]

When we connect with our gay neighbors, friends and the like, know that God is already at work in them, calling and wooing them to himself through the prevening work of the Holy Spirit. Our role then is to be attentive to what God is already doing in seeking to bring them to his Son, Jesus Christ, and join with him. God is the great evangelist; our job is to help our friends and neighbors connect the dots from these theophanies back to the very One to whom these experiences point to: God himself.

PRAY INTENTIONALLY

William Law once commented that there is nothing that makes us love a person so much as praying for them.[4] Prayer not only connects us with God on their behalf but changes our own hearts in relation to them. Do you want to learn to love your neighbors? Then start by praying for them.

Prayer is usually something we do rather spontaneously and therefore often without a lot of forethought or intentionality. If we are not careful, when we pray for those we don't know very well, we easily run the risk of praying out of all those faulty assumptions we forget we are carrying around. We get caught up praying *our* priorities for people, according to *our* posture toward them, not necessarily God's!

A woman I met at a conference told me that she was praying faithfully for a gay guy at her work and wanted to know what else she could do. (I get these kinds of questions all the time.) I casually asked her what sort of things she was praying for. Her immediate answer was that God would break up the gay relationship he was in. I pushed a little further, asking how well she knew her work colleague and whether she had ever met his partner. "Oh, not very well," she said about her colleague, and regarding his partner "Oh, I've only met him once when he came by the office."

I discovered in our conversation (as did she) that her first *real* priority for her colleague was that his gay relationship would break up. In other words, his gay behavior would cease. These types of prayers reveal (at the very least) two things: first, that she was more concerned about him being gay than the fact that he didn't know and love Jesus. And second, that his homosexuality was in some way blocking his access to God. And she confessed to thinking exactly this, that God might not really accept him till he had changed. It is this cracked and damaging theology that lies beneath some of the ministries set up to make gay people straight. We should by now be clear about one thing: heterosexuality doesn't give a person a direct ticket to heaven, a relationship with Jesus Christ does.

When we pray for people, we must pray what we know is true of God and his character, which the Scriptures reveal. Romans states that *nothing*, absolutely nothing in the whole world, can separate us from the love of God in Christ Jesus (Romans 8:38-39). And second, God never waits for us to get our lives "right" (whatever that might mean for any of us) before he extends his love toward us (Romans 5:8).

Since we met our neighbors with the "red door," I have changed my regular route when I go out in order to drive past their house. I do this for a couple of reasons: first, in case they are out walking their dogs, I can greet them; and second, so I can pray for them, for their home and for others who are part of their lives. Sometimes just a little more thought and intentionality about praying can change everything. Pray first and foremost that our gay neighbors would come to see the love and beauty of God in Jesus. That's our first priority. Whether they are in a gay relationship or not is not necessarily our business. Our business is to love, pray and serve, and let God sort out the rest.

LISTEN CAREFULLY

Christians are generally known to be "tellers" and not "listeners." But we can't lead, relate or love effectively without *truly* listening first. It is for good reason that Stephen Covey included the art of listening in his set of life-determining habits when he says that we should *seek first to understand and then to be understood.*[5] If we simply followed this advice, so much ungodly blather would be removed from the world, and we would have the benefit of living in a more civil society.

Novelist Flannery O'Conner once said that when addressing people who cannot or will not *hear*, one tends to shout.[6] It's not hard to hear the LGBT community shouting. They shout loud. And for the most part they are shouting at us because we are *not* listening. And when we do listen, we only hear anger and a whole lot of "attitude." We hear disrespect and even blasphemy against the church and God. We *hear* their sin. Filled with righteous indignation, we then become angry and lash back, fighting fire with fire, all the while feeling morally superior and justified. And with all this shouting back and forth we fail to hear what I believe is really being said.

One of the things that has always fascinated me about the LGBT community is the seeming disproportionate use of religious terms and imagery. Christian terms and themes are used to name anything from parties, bars, clubs, media and the like. One only needs to read gay newspapers to see what I mean. There are "Salvation" and "Resurrection" parties, "Virgin Mary" bars, "Redemption" clubs and so on. Gay pride marches always include some participants dressed as nuns and priests, and even one or two mock heads of prominent Christians displayed on platters. Now some of this disrespect can be put down to the obvious ongoing tussle between the two communities, but I think there is much more to it, something a whole lot more personal.

My friend Mark is one of those people who has a great gift of hospitality. He throws the most amazing dinner parties, gets out the best crockery, sets the table beautifully and makes people feel totally loved. On one particular night he had invited four gay couples to the home that Alan and I shared with him. We had a great dinner, and as the night wore on, the topic of conversation turned to what we all did for work, never an easy question, especially in this type of company, when you lead a church. Thankfully, they knew Mark was a Christian, so this didn't seem to surprise them. But the conversation that opened up from this point on became the surprise.

As people began to share, we discovered that no less than five out of the eight visitors that night had been actively involved in the church. Four of those said they had been raised as Christians. Statistically, this is way above the normal percentage we might expect from a subculture, particularly for Australia. Now, none of them were currently involved in church, nor did they have any intention; they had gotten the message loud and clear that the church (and by implication God and the gospel) was not for people like them.

As they opened up about their experiences, it was impossible not to get angry at the very church we represented. We found ourselves apologizing over and over again on behalf of both the church and a number of Christians we didn't even know! These are not unusual stories; the LGBT community is full of people who loved God but were rejected by a bigoted church.

The church is being yelled at. There is an enormous reservoir of pain and rejection among members of the LGBT community toward both God and the church. Some of this lies at the root of their collective shouting. They want to hurt because they have been hurt. Using Christian themes is both a conscious and unconscious way of getting back at the church. What might look like sacrilege is actually one of the means by which the LGBT community strikes back at a loveless church. And if we are to understand the power of the gospel itself, like all of our sins—except that of blasphemy against the Holy Spirit—it is totally forgivable (Mark 3:28-29). Why don't we who are forgiven much love much as Jesus says we should (Luke 7:47)?

In *Untamed* Alan and I talk about the importance of understanding something of the particular angst or collective pain that any given group may carry. It's hard to understand where the LGBT community is coming from, both socially and politically, without knowing something of their personal and collective stories. This surely includes the marginalization experienced from the church. Jean Vanier suggests that "true" listening is a gift to and for us, and includes knowing how to respect the wounds and sufferings of others.[7] The challenge before us is not to yell back but rather to listen more deeply. The Scriptures tell us that a *gentle* answer turns away wrath (Proverbs 15:1), not fighting fire with fire.

REPENT HUMBLY

Years ago our church in Australia ran a large conference on sexuality and related issues, including LGBT workshops. One of our key objectives was to break down homophobia and promote understanding in the church. Despite this, members of GLAD (Gays and Lesbians Against Discrimination) got wind of it and sent word out to their community to protest the conference. Their standard way of protesting at that time was to sneak in paint bombs and throw paint over the people and throughout the building.

By the time we were ready to start the conference there was standing-room only. People were packed in. GLAD protestors filled the first several rows inside the church, others were outside with their placards. The place looked like a circus. We had lesbians with their pit bull dogs(!), seven-foot transsexuals with feather boas, men wearing togas (no, I'm not joking), representatives from the media and the odd conservative Christian counselor not too sure of what to do and where to look! The tension in the room was clearly building, and they were ready for a fight.

We started by praying! Then our dear friend Sy Rogers, who was our keynote speaker, calmly walked to the microphone and welcomed everybody, especially the members of the LGBT community, for their presence. Not at all what they were expecting! He then addressed the Christians, asking for all those present who felt the gay community deserved an apology on behalf of the church to stand with him. All the Christians in the room stood up. You could have heard a pin drop! Sy then led us all in a heartfelt prayer of repentance for all the judgment, hostility and lack of love toward the LGBT community, both past and present.

Alan then stood up and said to the activists present that if they would give Sy his chance to speak (without interference), they could have full right of reply. In other words, they could have the microphone and present their case in response. It was such a powerful moment. Never had they encountered such a response. They had come looking for a fight and found instead a group of people who were willing to be humble enough to say sorry and give them the dignity of a voice. That night bridges were built and relational barriers broken down—all because of a simple "sorry." And in the midst of this they got to hear a powerful testimony to the difference Jesus makes in your life!

Our friends in Sydney have taken a similar approach and use the annual Gay Mardi Gras as an opportunity to publicly apologize. They form a group and march alongside LGBT people with placards and T-shirts with SORRY written across them.[8] They wanted the LGBT community to know that they were sorry, both personally and on behalf of the church. It is wonderful to see Andrew Marin's ministry in Chicago doing a similar thing.[9] Saying sorry doesn't mean one affirms everything another person does or believes; it simply acknowledges our sinful attitudes and actions in relating to them. This simple act has created significant relational opportunities between the two communities—all because a handful of Christians were willing to adopt a Christlike posture of humility.

Elton John sang years ago, "Sorry seems to be the hardest word."[10] It's so true. Why do we find it so hard to say? God's people should be the very ones marked by humility, repentance and, in turn, forgiveness. Even if we don't believe we have personally sinned against LGBT members, we sure belong to a historic church community that has. People who follow a humble God ought to have no problem in saying sorry when it is appropriate.

KNOCK KNOCK

The first step in loving any neighbor, and more specifically those we deem "different" from ourselves, is to look into our own hearts. How have we categorized them? What thoughts and attitudes have already been formed, perhaps with very little information? You will be surprised how much you already think you know about someone you haven't even yet met.

I believe if we start first by suspending our judgments, it will be easier to see God's image in the other. Look for the imago Dei and for the traces of God in their lives, pray more openly and intentionally, listen carefully, and repent humbly. This means *living* the good news of the gospel before we even get a chance to share it verbally. It's the old saying (attributed to St. Francis), "At all times preach the gospel. And when you have to, use words."

Do the LGBT community need to hear the gospel? You bet they do. Just like every other person who is yet to know Jesus. But perhaps they need to see it demonstrated in our very lives and actions first.

Re-Sexing the Church

God might have formed a perfect church; he chose,
instead, to establish one that was human.

JOHN HENRY NEWMAN

Having spent time around "sinners" and also around
purported saints, I have a hunch why Jesus spent so
much time with the former group: I think he preferred
their company. Because the sinners were honest about
themselves and had no pretense, Jesus could deal with
them. In contrast, the saints put on airs, judged him, and
sought to catch him in a moral trap. In the end it was the
saints, not the sinners, who arrested Jesus.

PHILIP YANCEY

I've always believed in an open table. Our big, square,
purple Communion table was set up right in the middle of our
gathering, symbolizing *Jesus*—not the band or the pulpit—as our
center. On the table were several large loaves of bread, bottled wine
and grape juice. The table was set low to the ground with cushions
scattered around so people could kneel or sit for as long as they

needed, and they did. Alone or with someone else, people came to meet with God, and many remained seated there until way after our gathering finished.

One of my most precious memories was captured one Sunday morning as I looked around that purple table. Sitting, breaking bread was a lady who had known Jesus her whole life. She was in her eighties, our oldest member, and dressed in her white lawn-bowling outfit. Right next to her sat a gay Jewish man in leather chaps. He was HIV positive and curious about Jesus. Among others was a woman (who had four kids) going through a very messy divorce, a speech pathologist who worked at a local hospital, and a former exotic dancer who had found Jesus in a strip club. As I watched them all, I wept. What a symbol of the broken, diverse body of Christ.[1]

Most people come to church because they are spiritually and relationally hungry. They come looking to connect with God and others. And if they don't feel welcome around the Communion table, how then will they eat? It's one of the few healing places where the broken can come, sit and partake. The broken body of Christ is reflected not just *on* the Communion table but also *around* the table. Isn't this what Communion is meant to symbolize?

> Certainly the Eucharist is as intimate as sex.
>
> **David Jensen**

A CHURCH MAKEOVER

One of the first things we did when we started in ministry was give our church building a loving "makeover." We saw the church as an extension of our home (and it was right next door) and wanted people to feel as comfortable as they would sitting in their own living rooms. This meant we ditched a lot of the more austere "religious" furniture, replacing it with sofas, cushions, art and the like, softening the space and making it feel more welcoming. We also let people bring food and drinks into the chapel area—something unheard of back then. We weren't just trying to be different, we merely wanted our gathering space to reflect who we were.

We soon discovered that a more relaxed church environment helps people *feel* more relaxed. Given the backgrounds of many of our people, this was really important. If they felt they needed to perform or to look a certain way, they wouldn't have come. Our folk needed to feel that no matter what else was going on in their lives, this was one place at least where they could be real. And no matter what issue they were struggling with they could be honest without risking rejection. Isn't this what we all long for?

Church environments are expressions of culture and communicate what we really believe. The vast majority of our church buildings are neat and tidy, sometimes bordering on sterile. Many churches I visit remind me of those perfect, somewhat lifeless, display homes where everything is clean, well-ordered and in its proper place.[2] Contrast this with the bloody altars in the Old Testament temple! Or the vibrant, very much lived-in houses (*oikos*) that formed the backbone of the New Testament church.

People are complex, and they experience life as somewhat more messy than what church culture typically communicates. Who really is going to risk introducing their personal mess into the perfectly ordered environments that make up so many of our churches? It becomes much easier to negotiate these places inauthentically, with our masks firmly in place. We can never truly be ourselves in lifeless environments. And so we become alienated from the church's message and experience profound loneliness in the crowd. Sexuality, that particularly messy aspect of our lives, once again gets caught up in this alienation.

Now I know that developing a welcoming environment takes more than just simply rearranging some furniture. I've been in comfortable environments that are still steeped in cultures of performance, expectation and exclusion. *Welcome* needs to be seen and felt on a number of levels, not just in how we decorate. To really understand the nature of hospitality and welcome, we need to rearrange both our family life and our community worship to be centered around the person of Jesus.

WHO IS MY MOTHER?

While I didn't learn a lot about sex from my mom, she did teach me many other things, but nothing has defined me quite as much as her sense of radical inclusiveness. She understood hospitality by growing up in a very full, welcoming house. People used to say of my Nana (Mom's mom) that she was a collector of stray dogs as well as stray people! And it was true. I still have vivid memories of her home; it was always full to the brim with people and animals! For my Nana (and my mom) there weren't any "outsiders"—everyone was able to find a place at the table.

Isn't that the point of the church? That anyone and everyone can find a place in Jesus (see Colossians 1:18-20 in *The Message*)? Yet if we fail to be welcoming around our own tables, then we're bound to fail at the broader church community level. And in order to expand our tables we need to take a long, hard look at our current, somewhat culturally conditioned, understanding of family.

Despite its rapid decline, the nuclear understanding of the family continues to define the middle-class sense of ideal family. A nuclear family is largely an independent unit sundered from a larger, more inclusive understanding of the extended family. Consisting of a mom, a dad, 2.5 kids, a pet, two cars, a home, a job that pays enough to send kids to college and so on, this configuration of family life (as the ideal) has dominated Western culture since the time of the post-Industrial Revolution, especially in the twentieth century.

But when you start caring for a child who is being adopted by a lesbian couple because his biological mom sold her body for drugs and no one even knows who his father is, then you have no choice but to reframe this "ideal" type of family. This is a new reality for many kids, like Jacob, who was our foster child. He, along with what is now a majority of people, does not live or experience the "normal" nuclear family unit.[3] Instead of seeing what could be a great opportunity for the church family to step into this void, we find ourselves too busy trying not to belong to each other, while frantically trying to prop up the nuclear family as the ideal family, believing if we could just get that right all our troubles would be resolved.

Now the problem is two-sided: On the one side, the nuclear family unit, only about a hundred years old, is failing. It's simply not working in and out of the church![4] It seems we simply do not thrive in nuclear family units, as the increasing divorce rates attest. On the other side, we are trying to prop up and resurrect a model of family that actually falls short of a biblical understanding. The Bible's concept of family is actually much larger than that of the diminishing nuclear family and is ultimately defined by our understanding of the *ecclesia*, the church.[5] The tragedy is that by taking a final stand on a narrowed understanding of family, Christians can inadvertently undermine the very work of the kingdom that they are seeking to advance.

Jesus' pointed question, "Who is my mother, my brother, my sister?" must have sounded shocking to Middle Eastern Jewish ears, to whom family was everything. Here was Jesus confounding them once again with radicalizing statements about the nature of the kingdom of God. What exactly did he mean? Surely he's not suggesting ditching his own family? This was (and is) a culture where biological bloodlines run as deep as any other. Families and family life are central to the Bible's understanding of blessing, covenant and lineage. No, he is not ditching family, but he is definitely enlarging it in rather surprising ways. I can't imagine how Mary must have felt when she heard this. This was her son! And trust me, I know how Jewish mammas can be—I married a Jew—sons are everything! Good Jewish boys don't go around calling their primary familial relationships and obligations into question. But that is exactly what Jesus does. Theologian Stanley Hauerwas is sensitive to these shifts, and notes that

To be a disciple of Jesus is to be made part of a new community in which the family is reconstituted. We are all
children, but now a community has been established in
which we are all called to be parents, brothers, and sisters to
and for one another. In such a community it is impossible
for an "unwanted child" to be born, for the biological family
has been transformed in service for the church. What is at
stake is not the family, but rather those who do the will of
the Father. For Jesus to take such a critical attitude toward
the family could not help but put him in tension with the
people of Israel. As a faithful son of Israel, Jesus was expected to marry and have a child. Yet Jesus remains single.
His singleness, moreover, is a sign that God's kingdom will
not grow by biological ascription. Rather, the kingdom of
God grows by witness and conversion. Through such growth
Christians will discover sisters and brothers we did not
know we had. Such is the wonder and the threat of the
kingdom brought in Christ.[6]

I'm not sure how all this fits with the oft-prescribed "God first,
family second, church third" that we evangelicals tend to repeat so
easily and so formulaically. Where does that come from anyway?
It's hard to square it with Jesus' absolute claim to our loyalties in
relation to family in Matthew 10:34-38. Jesus the prophet knew just
how easily familial attachment, blood lines, nationality and the like,
when cut off from the claims of the kingdom, could hinder the
cause of God in the world rather than advance it. This is why he
repeatedly drove this message home. Hauerwas observes,

Jesus has already challenged loyalty to family through the
calling of the disciples (Matt. 4:18-22), his refusal to let the
one desiring to be a disciple return to bury his father (8:18-22),
and his prediction that in the coming persecutions brother
will deny brother and fathers will rise up against their children

and children will put parents to death (10:16-23, 34-39). If there was any doubt that Jesus meant what he said, his identification of his true disciples as the disciples makes clear that his challenge to the family is radical.[7]

Authors like Janet Fishburne attribute much of the church's failure to engage society at large, particularly the poor and marginalized, as a direct result of our narrow vision of family: "Where the concerns of the nuclear family become the focus of a church, the conservation of middle-class ideals can blind both leaders and people to the prominent concern for social justice found in the Bible." She goes on to name this blindness as idolatry: "Family idolatry is a tragically misdirected form of religious devotion. It involves a preference for the familiar over the unknown, the local over the universal, and treats the familiar and local as if they were absolute."[8]

The missiological implications, as well as those relating to the vigor of church community, ought to be pretty clear.

NOT ON OUR SHIFT!

St. Martin's is a community church located in a complex part of town in Melbourne, Australia. They love and live alongside the predominantly poor and marginalized, and have lots of involvement with people who are in and out of prison. One Sunday morning Shirley (one of the beloved pastors) told the congregation that a woman who had been coming along, a young Christian, was facing prison time for previous offenses. The complex thing was that she had no other support structures, which meant her two children were facing being put into foster care. Shirley paused after reporting this and looked slowly and deliberately at the members of the congregation and said, "This will *not* happen on our shift! No child that is part of our community and extended family will ever be put into the foster care system. We are their brothers and sisters, parents, grandparents and guardians!" This is precisely the kind of the radical redefining of family that Jesus was talking about.

Who is my mother, my brother, my child, my grandma? These are difficult and confronting questions, yet each reader needs to wrestle personally with them. To be faithful, Jesus-loving families we need to ask ourselves how we can expand our circle of concern to include others. Each of us needs to broaden our tents, not narrow them (Isaiah 54:1-5). This will likely look different for all of us. For some families, they can do this through formal channels of adoption or fostering. Others can simply include singles or isolated elderly people into their homes and family life. We can all do this by sharing life as well as our homes. It's called Christian community, and it has a lot of healing magic in it.

My sister Sharon and her husband were one such family who took on this challenge. In a season in their lives when most young families turn inward (to raise children), they were very intentional about looking outward and including others into their family unit. They had many different people over the years share life with them. Two young, single, gay guys come to mind because they became affectionately known as the "third son" and the "fourth son." They all lived together (kids and all) and modeled a wonderful and different type of extended family.

They were just one of the many people in our church who did this. Al and I were married only one month before we had three singles move in with us. We encouraged our whole church community to do this, and they did! We ended up with all sorts of weird household configurations: singles with singles, families with singles, straight, gay, young, old—it didn't matter—and it worked! It was sometimes messy, but people really did learn to share lives and together helped one another along in their journey. Without even realizing it, we had, by our very lifestyles of welcome, redefined what a family is and what it can look like.

This seems to me to be particularly pertinent now in our current climate, not only with the breakdown of the nuclear family unit but with current statistics showing that singles (divorced, widowed, whoever and however one finds themselves single) are now the majority of people. Author Wesley Hill, a single gay man, highlights this as someone walking the path of celibacy, "Celibacy is a hard choice, and if churches are not willing to hold it up as an honorable pursuit and support it with practices of friendship and hospitality, I'm not sure it will seem viable to many sexual minorities." He adds, "The congregations that give me hope are ones where I see married people and single people, older people and younger people, all sharing meals and ministries and small groups together."[9]

This broader, more inclusive way of living and expanding our understanding of family is paramount if we are to truly understand the church as the family of God. I could tell story after story of people who "adopted" one another and redefined family—people who became aunts, brothers and grandpas. Something akin to the type of extended family Nelson Mandela depicts in his autobiography, *Long Walk to Freedom*. In one section he describes going to visit a neighboring village, saying that he never needed to call ahead or let them know he was coming, because he knew when he got there that "everyone was his mother, uncle, sister."[10]

Let's face it, when it comes to all this stuff, Jesus' words are pretty radical. While the implications can seem overwhelming, all it requires from us is a willingness to realign and enlarge our family life as a means of extending the kingdom. And that can begin with a few small but deliberate steps. It can be as simple as regularly inviting people for dinner, like that single mom at church, or the young gay guy who has just started coming. Learning to break bread with people that you wouldn't ordinarily is one first and very practical step. Who we have around our table says a lot about the Jesus we follow.

Jesus' words call us to a greater love, a greater commitment to the well-being of those within the household of God and beyond. It is sacrificial and costly. But it is this exact type of love expressed through God's people that others look at wide-eyed and say, "What type of love do these people have for one another?" It is this type of love that shows the world the reality of God. My life has been rich beyond measure, in no small part due to the multitude of weird and wonderful people who I have had the privilege of sharing life with.

Lesslie Newbigin famously said,

> I have come to feel that the primary reality of which we have to take account in seeking for a Christian impact on public life is the Christian congregation. How is it possible that the gospel should be credible, that people should come to believe that the power which has the last word in human affairs is represented by a man hanging on a cross?
>
> I am suggesting that the only answer, the only hermeneutic of the gospel, is a congregation of men and women who believe it and live by it. I am, of course, not denying the importance of the many activities by which we seek to challenge public life with the gospel—evangelistic campaigns, distribution of Bibles and Christian literature, conferences, and even books such as this one. But I am saying that these are all secondary, and that they have power to accomplish their purpose only as they are rooted in and lead back to a believing community.[11]

RE-JESUSING THE CHURCH

If we so easily erect walls around our family and family life, it makes sense that we do the same thing in our churches. We might get exposed to a little more diversity on a Sunday, when the larger family gathers, but we don't really want to have to deal with somebody who is a little strange, too different or somewhat out of the box. Which is why most of our churches are full with people who look just like us! We like our church to reflect our culture. That's why we have (often inadvertently) constructed sometimes arbitrary cultural and theological indicators of who is in and who

is out. I am going to suggest that most of our churches are structured around what social set theorists call "bounded sets."

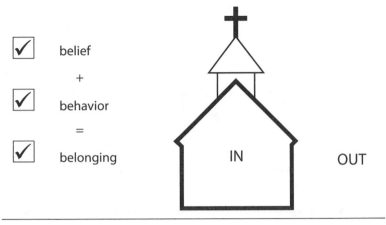

✓ belief

    +

✓ behavior

    =

✓ belonging   IN   OUT

Figure 11.1. Bounded-set church.

In figure 11.1 we have a bounded set as applied to the church. We
see a clear boundary (wall) around who is in and who is out. One's
inclusion, *belonging,* is based on how aligned one's *beliefs* and *behaviors* are with those on the inside. Some diversity (initially at
least) might be tolerated but is frowned upon over the long term.
In other words, greater conformity equates to greater acceptance,
continued resistance to prescribed belief or behavior usually leads
to some form of rejection.

Consider how so many churches tend to operate like this. The
mission of those on the inside is seen as going out to those on the
outside (defined as those who don't believe or behave like us), telling
them about Jesus, and hopefully bringing them in and getting them
believing and behaving correctly—like us. They will get *in* based
primarily on evidence of conformity to the accepted beliefs and behaviors of the host church. There is not a lot of room for diversity of
opinion or behavior. Here the primary concern is with conformity
to beliefs and practices. Bounded sets can be described as hard at
the edges and soft at the center.[12]

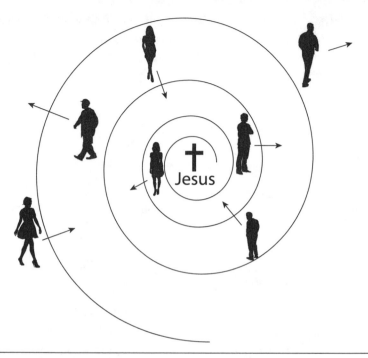

Figure 11.2. Centered-set church.

The centered set, on the other hand, has a "hard," well-articulated and vibrant theological center, but tends to be "soft" at the edges. It assumes that every person is *somewhere* in relation to the center—in this case, Jesus. One's relation to the center has to do with orientation, not necessarily closeness (as fig. 11.2 depicts). In other words, no matter how far away people might be from Jesus, they only need turn toward him (orientation) and he is right there. (God is not far from any of us [Acts 17:27-28].) Others who appear close might actually be looking away. While the concept of conversion is important in the centered set, people are seen as moving along a continuum toward the center, and conversion is seen as a process (embedded in discipleship) rather than simply a singular event.[13] The primary concern of those operating within this type of thinking is to orient others toward the Center. In other words, focusing them toward an authentic encounter and understanding of God in Jesus Christ.[14]

In contrasting the two we see that when Jesus is placed at the center *he*, not our cultural expressions or beliefs, becomes the primary focus. It's a shift from a more regulatory environment to one of direction toward a Person. Rules must not be allowed to get in the way of the primary relationships with Jesus; this must come first. Making Jesus central is vital for the very spiritual life of the congregation (Revelation 1–3), but it has huge implications for our missional effectiveness as well. Besides, substituting the checking of boxes (doctrinal or moral) for active relationship with Jesus always leads toward a coercive and controlling religion. As a consequence, "As was the case with the Pharisees in Jesus' day, the church has to a significant extent become the promoters and defenders of the very thing from which Christ came to free us," as Greg Boyd rather wryly notes.[15]

> Jesus calls men, not to a new religion, but to new life.
>
> Dietrich Bonhoeffer

A wonderful modern-day parable that depicts the difference between the bounded- and centered-set approaches is captured for us in an encounter between a farmer and a Japanese tourist in the Australian outback. The tourist is taken aback with the sheer vastness of the outback and comments to the farmer that as far as he can see, he can't see any fences. The tourist asks the farmer how he can possibly keep his sheep in without fences. The farmer replies that they don't need to build fences, they just dig wells and the sheep don't wander very far.

If people really drink from the well of *living water*, I believe they won't wander very far. Even my (now atheist) friend who used to be a Jesus follower can't quite walk too far away from Jesus; many of his blogs and Facebook posts are about Christianity. In fact, I believe part of his problem in the first place was that he was introduced to Jesus in a bounded-set church, where there was no place to wander or ask questions. I believe he has a thirsty heart and will eventually wander back to the Well.

JESUS: THE CENTER OF EVERYWHERE

This centered-set approach more accurately describes the approach that Jesus adopted in his own life and ministry. Just take a look at the ragtag bunch of folks that hung around him in those three world-changing years that were his ministry. Most of them didn't have a clue who they were dealing with! Few had a clearly articulated theology; they were believers, doubters, ex-terrorists, prostitutes and a betrayer. They were probably, like Jesus, accused of being gluttons and drunkards (Matthew 11:19). Yet here is Jesus putting himself at the center of their lives. He trusts himself and his message into the hands of these types of people!

> There is someone that I love, even though I don't approve of what he does. There is someone I accept, though some of his thoughts and actions revolt me. There is someone I forgive, though he hurts the people I love the most. That person is me.
>
> C. S. Lewis

I have no doubt some of their beliefs and behaviors would have put them outside many of our churches. But Jesus lets them continue to hang around, he lets them follow because he understands the importance of process, and honors each person's individual and unique journey of discipleship. Levi's particular journey to Jesus was totally different from John's, as was Peter's from Judas's. As is yours and mine; we've got to get to Jesus to get to God, but we all come from different contexts, and our narratives vary widely.

Jesus himself seems to critique the bounded-set approach when he addresses the Pharisees in Matthew 23. "You are like whitewashed tombs, which look beautiful on the outside but on the inside are full of the bones of the dead and everything unclean" (v. 27). Here were the "righteous" ones, those who believed and behaved in all the right ways, yet their hearts were far from God. Pharisaism was a very defined bounded set.

If we had to be honest, there exists a Pharisee in each of us. We all pretend in some way that we've got it all together, and if we can't convince ourselves then we want to at least be able to convince others. And the bounded set provides at least some clear markers. But when these markers become entrenched as indicators of acceptance, tools to indicate how well others are performing, then we have in effect set up a counterfeit religion.

Perhaps our own fear of failure and lack of grace toward ourselves cause us to want a say in who is in and who is out, and this is one of the reasons I think the bounded set has such strong appeal. Jesus tells the famous parable of the wheat and the tares (Matthew 13:24-30) to make this precise point—that we simply cannot know who's really in and who's really out until the closing of the messianic age. And even then, according to Jesus in another place (Matthew 25), there are going to be a lot of surprises on that day. Winners and losers will take on a whole different look. Jesus does this all the time with his parables about the least, the lost and the last (as well as embodied in him being a friend of sinners [Luke 7:34; 15:2]). These are not called the Great Reversals for nothing!

SEX AND SETS

Now some of you at this stage might be thinking, *What has all this stuff about structures and extending our families got to do with sexuality?* Well, in some ways everything. Sexuality, not restricted to genital expression, is the social neighbor-facing equivalent to the spirituality that characterizes our relationship to God: our need to know and be known, love and be loved by the other. And isn't the church (as the body of Christ) the primary context where relationships are lived and played out? This is where we learn how to relate, how to love, how to forgive and be forgiven, how to give and receive grace.

If the very nature of our sexuality is to search, to be curious, to want to connect, then it is no surprise to me (or God, for that matter) that in our quest we sometimes lose direction, take a side alley and fall short of God's best. In the centered set we always have a way back to Jesus, because he is the center to which we can and must always return. He is the judge, and to him we must give account. But he has also opened the path for us to enter his presence as his beloved people. Our judge is also our Redeemer-King. He will change us; that's what he does (Hebrews 1–6). The chief role of the church is to create the right environment for all people to be able to encounter Jesus; everything else that we do is relative to this great cause.

I finish this chapter with some of the characteristics (and there are surely many more) that mark a church who has Jesus at its center.

WELCOMING OF ALL

When Jesus is placed at the center, it means *all* people are welcome. That is the open invitation of our God. No matter where you are or where you have been, God welcomes you. But that God welcomes all (Matthew 11:28) does not necessarily mean that God affirms all that we human beings are up to. In fact the whole purpose of the gospel is to address the problem of human sin and brokenness. This is the tricky bit when developing a centered-set community around Jesus, because when you take away the bounded set (along with the various regulations), it's a lot harder to navigate. This is why the center (Jesus is Lord) must be solid, and the leadership visibly committed to his highest standards of discipleship in the community. In my experience the more messy the community, the more the members seem to rely on the strength and conviction of the leadership.

I love the expression "welcoming and mutually transforming."[16] This to me sums up what the approach of the church should be. Are we to be welcoming of all people? Absolutely! Are we to affirm all belief systems and behaviors of all who break bread with us? Absolutely not. If God doesn't affirm all human behavior, then neither can his ecclesia. However, we need to be clear that Jesus and his way must take priority. And remember, he is not the standard religious kind of guy. He's unlikely to simply agree with you no matter where you stand on these matters.

Being welcoming and mutually transforming moves the issue from just being about LGBT people to being about *all* people. I have never been one for developing specific church policies on homosexuality. If we have a policy on homosexuality, why wouldn't we also develop policies about every other ethical issue? For instance, what is our policy about greed? Jesus seems pretty concerned about this, yet I don't know a single church who has a formal policy on it. The problem with writing policies on a particular issue is that you make *that* issue more important than the others; then we're back to our totem pole and our bounded set.

PRIESTLY IN OUR ROLE

Digging wells instead of building fences invites us to cultivate a much more dynamic awareness and relationship with Jesus. We learn to live into the truths of Ephesians 1, where Jesus is rightfully seen to be the absolute epicenter of the church's life and worship. This is a much more untamed and vibrant way of following Jesus than living by the domestic familiarity and rules of the bounded set.

In living this way it's necessary to see ourselves fundamentally as priests. At core, a priest is someone who mediates the knowledge of God. They represent God to the people and the people to God. This role lies at the core of every believer's identity and function in the world. We are all called to priestly activity; all of us are called to introduce people to God (i.e., point them to Jesus), and then at some point we need to get out of the way. This doesn't mean that we don't encourage, nurture and correct at times, but it does mean we have to let go of control and let people journey in a way that makes sense to them and where they are at with God.

In *Untamed,* Alan tells how this truth became very personally evident to us. As you might imagine, our early years of ministry were pretty chaotic. We were dealing with many people whose lives were profoundly broken. We had a major ministry among the street prostitutes of our city. In caring for them we had somehow operated in the belief that it was part of our pastoral responsibilities to directly help them make right choices, to correct their lives and put them back on track. In other words, we had taken the path of the control freak. Bad decision! The problem is that the brokenness we were dealing with was so profound that it seemed to be an impossible task. Consequently, we were always on the edge of burnout.

One day, when lying in a near fetal position in pre-burnout stress, Al felt a challenge from God that his core task with people was to be a priest. It went something like this:

GOD   Well then, Alan, let's test your theological skills. What do priests do?

ALAN   Lord, they introduce people to God and God to people. Aren't they also meant to mediate a true knowledge of God?

GOD   Good enough. Well, get to it then!

The challenge was for him to do precisely this: introduce Sarah the hooker to Jesus (a right presentation of him) and introduce Jesus to Sarah, and then get out the way. This was so life-changing to my dear husband because he realized that Jesus is so much better at changing people than he is. In fact, Al says that when he tried to play Holy Spirit, he always bungled it (funny that!). The truth is that none of us are meant to do what only God can do. We simply have to guide people to Jesus, and he will do all that is necessary to restore them to the image of God. Redemption and sanctification is his job, not ours.

Of course there will be times when we play a more direct role in people's lives, but we must realize that it is always temporary and reflective of what Jesus is doing in them. We cannot force the agenda. Galatians is very clear about this; we are called to bear one another's burdens, and by doing so we fulfill the law of Christ. But the same verses say that each should also bear their own load (Galatians 6:1-5). This is what growing up in Christ is: we move from needy dependence to mutual interdependence. We let go of any crutches and other artificial supports, and learn to walk on our own two feet. Grownups, mature believers, know what it is to have a relationship with the living Christ. They are not bound by the law but are set free by Jesus to live and be all that he calls them to be.

SANCTIFICATION IS A JOURNEY

Centered-set thinking allows everyone to journey to Jesus in his or her own unique way, and we all end up perfectly unique in him (1 John 3:2; 2 Corinthians 3:18). While we all might be heading in the same direction, our paths are different and we journey at a different pace. Discipleship in a bounded-set context can tend to look like some sort of cookie-cutter spiritual production line where everyone gets processed in the same way and at the same time. But we know from life and experience that nothing is further from the truth. I might be dealing with anger, while you might be dealing with lust and others with shame. In some ways you might be further ahead than me, and in other areas I will lead you. Our stories are so different, our personalities so particular, and our lives so complex that only God will know how to heal us (and deal with us) without destroying who we are uniquely. Discipleship in a centered set is more true to reality, gives more room to move, and honors the uniqueness of the person, their journey and particular angle of that journey. Being remade into the image of God in Christ is the most personal process imaginable, not some cookie-cutter process where we all end up looking the same.

I've already introduced you to Jasmine (who adopted Al and me as her mom and dad). Jasmine used to come with me every now and again when I would talk at churches and sometimes would share her story of what it was like being a transgender woman. One morning after a service around coffee, a lady (she even looked like the "Church Lady")[17] came straight up to me wanting to know why Jasmine had not gone back to being a man. Her question was understandable, but as we progressed I sensed it was also about her own discomfort with people like Jasmine.

In a bounded set we really like things to be neater than what they often are in reality. People like Jasmine are outside the box for most people, and we really don't know what to do with them. Did God make a mistake with Jasmine's biological sex? I don't think so. I think there are many complex and painful reasons why she now lives as a woman, and for people to suggest that she needs to go back to being a man is simplistic, to say the least. What this lady didn't know was that two previous churches had tried to insist on this, and on one occasion Jasmine tried to hang herself. To re-embrace a masculine identity was for her simply too painful.

In many ways Jasmine is further ahead than others in some areas of sanctification. For instance, she is one of the most self-giving servants I have ever met. It is never a problem for her to give up time to clean someone's house as a gift. She is generous to a fault; she wouldn't even think twice about giving all her money away to someone in need, and she doesn't have much to begin with. She really is a remarkable servant. What the "Church Lady" could not see or understand was that there are many areas in Jasmine's life where there has been remarkable healing. She has forgiven people she didn't think she could. She is living an independent life that she wasn't able to before. She hasn't been admitted to a psych hospital for many years. She doesn't take drugs, nor does she abuse alcohol or sell her body anymore. All these things are indicators of significant growth. Why didn't these matter in the church lady's assessment of Jasmine? We need to be very careful with these things.

Jasmine's story is not *my* story, and is definitely different from the story of the lady who challenged me. Jasmine is a unique child of God, and by God's grace she will make her way Home, even if it is as a woman.

Sometimes we have expectations of people that they just can't fulfill. And yet God accepts them anyway. This doesn't let any of us off the hook, for we are all called to press into God, but it does mean we have to be very sensitive to those in our midst that simply can't "perform" in the ways we want or think they should. Nonetheless we are all headed toward Jesus—we simply hold each other accountable to stay on that journey.

ACCEPTANCE PRECEDES REPENTANCE

Romans 2:4 reminds us that God's kindness leads us to repentance, not God's harshness or the wagging of the finger, but kindness. This is one of the cornerstones of our understanding of the gospel, that while we were yet enemies Christ died for us (Romans 5:8). None of us make it because we have our act together. It is all grace from the beginning to the end.

One of the most beautiful examples of the kindness of God in Jesus in seen in John 8:1-11, the story of Jesus and the woman caught in adultery. Here is a wonderful demonstration of both God's grace and acceptance. Here is a woman caught in the act of adultery. Incidentally, where was the adulterous man? If she was caught in the act, he had to have been there as well. Why didn't they drag him into the crowds? (One does wonder!) Anyhow, she was more than likely naked in front of a leering crowd of religious men (think Taliban here and you can get a feel for the situation). I can't even imagine how she must have been feeling. This woman is facing death; her fear and terror eclipsing her humiliation. And her fate lay in the outcome of this encounter between this mysterious man Jesus and the religious leaders.

He begins by restoring something of her dignity; he moves the focus from her to the crowd and then looks down to the ground. He asks them to search their own hearts. The leering men were sinning by participating in the naked violence of the moment. He then exposes their hypocrisy, thereby putting everyone on the same level. This was not what the crowd was anticipating. The Pharisees, the religious elites, were put in the same category as an adulterer! I love Jesus even more for this! Don't you?

After all the men had gone, Jesus then speaks words of life to her, words of remarkable acceptance: "Woman, I do not condemn you." This is what it means to have direct access to Jesus. We are accepted first. And then in the context of his acceptance (his kindness) we are able to repent. I believe that Jesus was very intentional in the way he ordered his words. He offered her access to himself. Knowing that he was the living water, he was the only one who could quench her thirst. Once she knows this, he then tells her to sin no more. Acceptance preceded repentance. This is the type of redemptive love Jesus models for us, the kind he expects we will have for one another. The problem is that we often get it the other way around. We expect people to repent first, then we'll accept them. Leave that behavior or that sin, get this cleaned up, fix that, then you can belong.

IN ESSENTIALS UNITY, IN NONESSENTIALS LIBERTY, IN ALL THINGS LOVE

If one of the defining characteristics of the bounded set is conformity, then it stands to reason that the centered set will be characterized by diversity. And that diversity might manifest in a number of ways.

The formula "In essentials unity, in nonessentials liberty, in all things love," ascribed to Augustine, is in fact precisely what a centered set aims at achieving. Resist the age-old religious temptation to make nonessentials essential and make essentials nonessential. Essentials take us to our deepest theological truths (i.e., the Trinity, the person and work of Jesus, the resurrection, the authority of Scripture, etc.). Churches wanting to engage society with a gospel witness will need to recover a sense of what is essential and what is not.

Much of our quibbling is around nonessentials, and our disagreements are seldom done in love. Christians seldom allow people to disagree without wishing them to conform to their own standards. For instance, I do drink alcohol because my conscience is absolutely clear about it. But if my drinking causes someone with an authentic vulnerability to alcohol to stumble, I will definitely refrain. But this ought to work both ways; for those who abstain for whatever reasons, I expect that they give me (and others they might disagree with) the same grace afforded them. It's amazing to me that we have whole denominations making this an essential issue of fellowship when it is clearly a nonessential issue in the Bible. Some Christians use medical marijuana to help with stress and other ailments. The deep irony is lost on the very people who soundly condemn them who pop manufactured pharmaceuticals (e.g., antidepressants, pain-killers, anti-nausea, etc.) without any ethical qualms at all. And then of course there is the age-old issue of worship style or preference. I just met people deeply committed to *a capella* church (churches that refuse to use any musical instruments in their churches) and who believe that to use a guitar or a piano in worship is being disobedient. Churches like this refuse to fellowship with other disciples based on some obscure historical and cultural predilection. I have to admit that this utterly baffles me.

I could go on. If you have been around the church for anytime at all you will be all too aware of how trivial we religious people can be. Don't make nonessentials essential. Recognize instead that we are all different; we have different stories, DNA and cultures, and we all at some point have to stand before God and give an account for the way we lived. I personally am trusting that God will be kind and gracious to me as I try to be obedient and honor him from within whatever knowledge of him that I have. And I hope that this is true for you. You don't want to be judged on the various quirks of your theology and behavior, whatever they may be. It's simply not my (or your) right to judge how other people have journeyed, only that they have somehow remained in the Way and have become more like their Lord and Savior, Jesus.

I'm very grateful that I belong to a community that actively values diversity. Actually, we not only value diversity, we really *love* it as fundamental to God's ecclesia (cf. Revelation 21). It is a community that will *not* shut you out simply because you have a different opinion. For example, on the issue of homosexuality our church has the full gamut of opinion, but it does not divide us. In fact, one of our members, a dear friend, Paul, while having different conclusions (on LGBT issues, theologically speaking) has been the one to support my writing of this book every step of the way. He doesn't allow this to divide our essential fellowship in Jesus, and neither do I. And the point is, we don't have to! When respect and dignity is afforded the other, diversity is its reward.

LEAN TOWARD GRACE

I was teaching on this and the centered-set approach, and was challenged by someone in the audience. They simply couldn't get their head around it. It seemed way too messy for them and seemed to play too lightly with God's grace and had too low a view of the law. Yet, while it seems counterintuitive, I actually find the opposite to be true. Listen to pastor and author Tullian Tchividjian on this:

> Christians who talk a lot about grace are thought to have a low view of God's law. Correspondingly, those with a high view of the law are thought to be legalists. But the late Presbyterian theologian J. Gresham Machen said this gets the matter backwards: "A low view of the law always produces legalism; a high view of the law makes a person a seeker after grace." This is because a low view of the law encourages us to conclude that

we can keep it—the bar is low enough for us to jump over. A low view of the law makes us think that its standards are attainable, its goals reachable, its demands doable. . . .

This means that, contrary to what some Christians would have you believe, the biggest problem facing the church today is not "cheap grace" but "cheap law"—the idea that God accepts anything less than the perfect righteousness of Jesus. . . . A high view of the law reminds us that God accepts us on the basis of Christ's perfection, not our progress.[18]

If you doubt this, then does not Galatians 2:21 tell us that if we could be saved by the law then there was no point in Jesus' coming (cf. Romans 6:15-18)? In the end the law points us beyond itself to the one who embodies it within himself. He fulfilled it on our behalf. When we are compelled and motivated by Jesus instead of rules and regulations, then we are motivated by grace and not guilt. And grace is a far greater motivator than the law ever was.

I am reminded of Max Lucado's response when asked if preaching grace might encourage sin. He acknowledges that that might be true for a time, especially if someone is reacting to a rules-based religion. But he says that when a person truly experiences grace, he or she will experience Jesus, and that must lead to positive change, for to encounter grace is to encounter God in Jesus—and that means change.[19] I have found that when people truly encounter the power of grace, the sheer costliness of it all, they will come to understand *response*-ability in its truest sense. A disciple lives in response to God's high grace—this is the meaning of freedom and righteousness in Jesus.

Conclusion

The Climax

I'm not sure about other authors, but I imagined that by the time I got to this stage of the book I would be filled with a great sense of relief. And in some ways I am. But I am also filled with a strange sense of anxiety, even dread, knowing that once my thoughts are in print, that's it—they can't be taken back. As a speaker I'm used to having an audience in front of me, where I can *see* you and you can *see* me. In a book I can't engage you in quite the same way. Nor can I expand, qualify or easily retract my words. You don't get to see or feel the nuance, complexity or inner tension that I carry around some of these issues. This makes print feel so darn final.

It feels entirely right that this conclusion is being written on a visit back to Australia, where at least ten years ago I first felt the call to write. It also seems appropriate that while writing this conclusion I was interrupted by a FaceTime call from Jasmine, our "adopted" daughter. People like Jasmine really are gifts from God for all of us because they confront us with all of our assumed certainties. They in so many ways *are* our prophetic challenge. They dare us to love, to move beyond our cloistered, churchy worlds to embrace the weird and wonderful world we find ourselves in. My experience is that this is exactly where we can always find Jesus. Just read the Gospels.

We have now come to a place where our own appreciation of the power of the gospel, and how it relates to our world is inextricably bound up with how we deal with the marginalized and rejected people in our culture. It was the same for the religious in the time of Jesus. Jesus must show us the way yet again.

But it's not only the prophetic (and missional) challenge that confronts us. It's also about our own fear of and lack of understanding of our own sexuality—ourselves. We have to simply admit that Christian spiritual traditions of the West have *not* formed us well in this area. It is as if we have been left stranded on the shores of the twenty-first century as underdeveloped, oversexed adolescents attempting to navigate adult bodies in a deeply sexualized context.

The poet Rainer Maria Rilke likewise laments our own sense of immaturity in coming to grips with the humanizing power of our sexuality:

> Why, if guilt or sin had to be invented because of the inner tension of the spirit, why did they not attach it to some other part of our body, why did they let it fall on *that* part, waiting till it [guilt] dissolved in our pure source and poisoned and muddied it? Why have they made our sex homeless, instead of making it the place for the festival of our competency?[1]

Given that sexuality is core to our humanity and intrinsically connected to our spirituality, it is essential for our growth and maturity that we learn how to have naked conversations about sexuality and spirituality. We need to not only talk, discuss and debate, but integrate sexuality into our lives, our bodies, and ultimately into the living body of Christ.

Early in the book I suggested that G. K. Chesterton was on cue when he said that a man knocking on the door of a brothel was in fact looking for God. It's interesting that Freud was thought to have said in response that in going to church one was looking for sex.[2] While he might have meant it more polemically (he had a profound contempt for religion), he was right in naming the direct correlation between the search for God and human sexuality. As we have seen in section one, religion, our sustained quest for God in the world and community, is saturated with sexual metaphor, inarticulate longings, burning desires for connection, the need for healing relationship, the search for true identity and so on. In other words, it cannot be divorced from our sexuality. This is what it means to be fully human.

I offer this book in all humility, and pray my words are received in the spirit they are intended. Words on a page can only go so far, for sexuality is deep and complex, but I trust the Lord will use my small offering to further advance his kingdom and unity of the body. And that you (and he) will forgive me when I speak out of line!

My husband said to me upon first reading the manuscript of this book, "You really are pushing grace to just about as far as you can take it." Which of course raises the question, How far does grace go? And at the end of the day that really is one of the fundamental questions we are all wrestling with.

> "Return to your home, and declare how much God has done for you." And he went away, proclaiming throughout the whole city how much Jesus had done for him. (Luke 8:39 ESV)

Acknowledgments

First and foremost I want to thank my adorable husband, Alan. You have been my guide, my agitator, my greatest critic and my greatest encourager. Without you this book simply would not be written. Sharon and Mark—this is our story! Thanks, too, to my mum and dad and incredible family, who have encouraged me every step of the way, and to my pastor Pat, whose love and grace continue to define me. And thanks be to God, without whom there would be no story.

My deep gratitude goes to those who let me share their stories in the book. And special mention to some old and dear friends with whom so much of this story involved: Maz, Rob, Simon and Sy, and our other comrades in the Purple Heart team. Thanks also to the multitude of dear ones who have shared their stories with me over the years, and those who have sat in one of my classes, especially my YITS students. Thank you, each of you, for the song your life sings.

And big thanks to the fabulous Dave Zimmerman. Outside of my husband you had to deal most with the ravings of a crazy lady, and you did it ever so well. This book would certainly not be intelligible if not for your eloquent pen. And to all at IVP for your love and support, especially Andrew Bronson, Adrianna Wright, Cindy Bunch and Drew Blankman. You are all amazing!

Notes

INTRODUCTION: FOREPLAY

[1]Alan Hirsch and Debra Hirsch, *Untamed: Reactivating a Missional Form of Discipleship* (Grand Rapids: Baker, 2010).

CHAPTER 1: OH MY GOD! SEXUALITY MEETS SPIRITUALITY

[1]Jeffrey Kluger, "The Power of Love," *Time*, January 19, 2004, p. 64, quoted in Christopher West, *Theology of the Body for Beginners: A Basic Introduction to Pope John Paul II's Sexual Revolution* (West Chester, PA: Ascension Press, 2004), p. v.

[2]M. Scott Peck, *Further Along the Road Less Travelled* (New York: Touchstone, 1998), p. 220.

[3]Shmuley Boteach, *Kosher Sex: A Recipe for Passion and Intimacy* (London: Duckworth, 1998), p. 105.

[4]West, *Theology of the Body*, p. 55.

[5]See *Life Positive*, www.lifepositive.com/body/sexuality/sex-spirituality.asp.

[6]Not surprisingly, the actual physiological experience of "the little death" is actually caused by the release of *oxytocin* in the brain after the occurrence of the orgasm. A recent study of brain activation patterns using *positron emission tomography* (PET) give some support to the experience of a small death: "To some degree, the present results seem to be in accordance with this notion, because female orgasm is associated with decreased blood flow in the *orbito-frontal cortex*, a part of the brain that is crucial for behavioural control" (J. Georgiadis et al., "Regional Cerebral Blood Flow Changes Associated with Clitorally Induced Orgasm in Healthy Women," *European Journal of Neuroscience* 24, no. 11 [2006]: 3305-16).

[7]Alan Hirsch and Debra Hirsch, *Untamed: Reactivating a Missional Form of Discipleship* (Grand Rapids: Baker, 2010), p. 213.

[8]Ibid., p. 214.

[9]"Entry for Strong's 3045," www.studylight.org/lex/heb/view.cgi?number =03045.

[10]James Nelson, cited in Jim Cotter, *Pleasure, Pain and Passion: Some Perspective on Sexuality and Spirituality* (Sheffield, UK: Cairns Publication, 1993), p. 3.

[11]Cole Porter, "Let's Do It (Let's Fall in Love)," 1928.

[12]West, *Theology of the Body*, pp. 1-2.

[13]N. T. Wright, *Simply Christian: Why Christianity Makes Sense* (New York: HarperCollins, 2006), p. vi. The four areas that he talks about are (1) the human

longing for justice, (2) the quest for spirituality, (3) the hunger for relationships and (4) the delight in beauty.

[14]Ibid., p. 29.

[15]Cotter, *Pleasure, Pain and Passion*, pp. 3-4.

CHAPTER 2: MODESTY GONE MAD

[1]Historians record that Origen's prime motivation in doing this was so that he could tutor women without any suspicion.

[2]Carmen Renee Berry, *The Unauthorized Guide to Sex and the Church* (Nashville: Thomas Nelson, 2005), p. 80.

[3]It's interesting that this dualistic understanding in the Greek culture caused some to refrain from pleasures and others to overindulge. Christianity clearly took the refraining or abstinence road.

[4]Natalie Trust, "We Can't Be Friends Because We Might Have Sex," *Natalie Trust* (blog), http://natalietrust.com/?p=826.

[5]"Profile America: Facts for Features," US Census Bureau, www.census.gov /newsroom/releases/archives/facts_for_features_special_editions/cb12-ff18 .html and "American Families and Living Arrangements: 2011," Table A1, US Census Bureau, www.census.gov/population/www/socdemo/hh -fam/cps2011 .html.

[6]Dan Brennan, *Sacred Unions, Sacred Passions: Engaging the Mystery of Friendship Between Men and Women* (Elgin, IL: Faith Dance, 2010), p. 42.

[7]Ibid., pp. 56-57.

[8]Ibid., p. 57.

[9]Wendy Shalit, *A Return to Modesty: Discovering the Lost Virtue* (New York: Touchstone, 1999), pp. 85, 104.

[10]Havelock Ellis, quoted in ibid., p. 1.

[11]Ted Peters, *Sin: Radical Evil in Soul and Society* (Grand Rapids: Eerdmans, 1949), p. 26.

[12]Michael Frost and Alan Hirsch, *The Faith of Leap: Embracing a Theology of Risk, Adventure and Courage* (Grand Rapids: Baker, 2011), p. 85.

[13]John Piper, "Twelve Questions to Ask Before Watching 'Game of Thrones,'" *Desiring God*, June 20, 2014, www.desiringgod.org/blog/posts/12-questions-to-ask -before-you-watch-game-of-thrones.

[14]Gregory A. Boyd, *Repenting of Religion: Turning from Judgment to the Love of God* (Grand Rapids: Baker, 2008), p. 103.

[15]Alan Hirsch and Debra Hirsch, *Untamed: Reactivating a Missional Form of Discipleship* (Grand Rapids: Baker, 2010), p. 224. See also Branko Milanovic, "True World Income Distribution," *Economic Journal* 112 (2002): 51-92, http:// schmidt-bremen.de/mgm/True_Income_distribution_world.pdf. The research also finds that assets of $2,200 per adult placed a household in the top half of the world wealth distribution in the year 2000. To be among the richest 10 percent of adults in the world required $61,000 in assets, and more than

$500,000 was needed to belong to the richest 1 percent, a group which—with 37 million members worldwide—is far from an exclusive club. Most of us easily fit into the top 10 percent.

[16]Richard Rohr, "'New Fundamentals' Are a Contradiction in Terms," *Richard Rohr's Daily Meditations*, June 16, 2013, http://myemail.constant contact.com/Richard-Rohr-s-Daily-Meditations---New-Fundamentals--Are -a-Contradiction-in-Terms----Ecumenism----Father-s-Day--June-16--2013 .html?soid=1103098668616&aid=Hfqy-qPpvFQ.

[17]Lauren Winner, *Real Sex: The Naked Truth About Chastity* (Grand Rapids: Brazos, 2005), p. 30.

[18]Walter Brueggemann, *Genesis*, Interpretation (Atlanta: John Knox Press, 1982), p. 46

[19]Gregory A. Boyd, *Repenting of Religion: Turning from Judgment to the Love of God* (Grand Rapids: Baker, 2004).

[20]Abraham Heschel, *A Passion for Truth* (London: Secker & Warburg, 1973), p. 52.

[21]Martin Buber, *Israel and the World: Essays in a Time of Crisis* (New York: Shocken Books, 1963), p. 18.

CHAPTER 3: JESUS . . . SEX SYMBOL?

[1]Michael Frost, *Longing for Love: Gender, Sexuality and Our Experience of God* (Sutherland, Australia: Albatross Books, 1996), p. 184.

[2]Marilyn Sewell, "The Sexuality of Jesus," *Huffington Post*, September 27, 2012, www.huffingtonpost.com/marilyn-sewell/the-sexuality-of-jesus_b_1915011 .html.

[3]Marva Dawn, *Sexual Character: Beyond Technique to Intimacy* (Grand Rapids: Eerdmans, 1993), p. 9. We will explore these terms more fully in chapter four.

[4]There are some who suggest the beloved disciple was someone other than John, but traditional church teaching has suggested that it is indeed John the disciple. See James D. Tabor, "Who Was the Mysterious 'Disciple Whom Jesus Loved'?" *TaborBlog*, August 20, 2012, http://jamestabor .com/2012/08/20/who-was-the-mysterious-disciple-whom-jesus-loved.

[5]John MacArthur, "John: The Apostle of Love," *Grace to You*, April 14, 2002, www.gty.org/resources/sermons/62-1.

[6]J. M. Miller, "The Friendships of Jesus," *Grace Gems*, 1897, http://gracegems .org/Miller/friendships_of_jesus.htm and "Personal Friendships of Jesus," *ManyBooks.net*, 1897, http://manybooks.net/titles/miller jr2734927349-8 .html#.

[7]Dan Brennan, *Sacred Unions, Sacred Passions: Engaging the Mystery of Friendship Between Men and Women* (Elgin, IL: Faith Dance, 2010), p. 111.

[8]This quote is attributed to Maya Angelou, but also to Max Lucado and Carol Wimmer. Source unknown.

[9]Jim Cotter, *Pleasure, Pain and Passion: Some Perspective on Sexuality and Spirituality* (Sheffield, UK: Cairns, 1988), p. 71.

[10]Felicity Dale, *The Black Swan Effect: A Response to Gender Hierarchy in the Church* (Seattle: CreateSpace, 2014), p. 93.

[11]See, for example, Ed Stetzer, "Ed Stetzer's Advice: Avoid Even a Hint," *Sermon-Central*, May 8, 2014, http://bit.ly/SRcJFE.

[12]Dawn, *Sexual Character*, p. 11, italics added.

[13]"Profile America: Facts for Features," US Census Bureau, www.census.gov /newsroom/releases/archives/facts_for_features_special_editions/cb12 -ff18.html.

[14]Jean Vanier, *Man and Woman He Made Them* (Strathfield, Australia: St. Paul Publications, 1985), pp. 115-16.

[15]Ibid., p. 116.

[16]Philip Yancey, *Rumors of Another World: What on Earth Are We Missing?* (Grand Rapids: Zondervan, 2003), p. 87.

[17]Albert Hsu, *Singles at the Crossroads* (Downers Grove, IL: InterVarsity Press, 1997), p. 178.

[18]Brennan, introduction to *Sacred Unions, Sacred Passions*.

CHAPTER 4: THE EIGHT FUNDAMENTALS OF SEX

[1]Marva Dawn, *Sexual Character: Beyond Technique to Intimacy* (Grand Rapids: Eerdmans, 1993).

[2]Judith and Jack Balswick, renowned sex therapists, also talk about these two primary ways of relating in their book *Authentic Human Sexuality: An Integrated Christian Approach* (Downers Grove, IL: IVP Academic, 2008). "Being created as sexual beings means we have physical capacity for erotic sexuality [*genital sexuality*], but generally our sexual energy gives us a vitality for relating to others that goes beyond our erotic instincts. The majority of gratifying relationships in our life are actually non-erotic, such as between parent and child, siblings, same-and-opposite-sex friendships, extended family members, significant others in our work environments, and in our small and large communities. These relationships deeply enrich and give meaning to our lives" (p. 74).

[3]Dawn, *Sexual Character*, p. 11.

[4]Ibid., p. 10.

[5]I don't want to diminish the pain/negativity some may feel related to bad experiences of sex/sexuality, I just want to affirm that sexuality is a good gift from God; his intent was never for it to be used and misused in the ways it has.

[6]A place recognized as somewhere to meet other men to have anonymous genital sexual encounters. See "Gay Beat," *Wikipedia*, http://en.wikipedia .org/wiki/Gay_beat.

[7]Leonard Sax, "Why Are So Many Girls Lesbian or Bisexual?" *Psychology Today*, April 3, 2010, www.psychologytoday.com/blog/sax-sex/201004

/why-are-so-many-girls-lesbian-or-bisexual.

[8]Catholic Theological Society of America, quoted in Stanley Grenz, *Sexual Ethics: A Biblical Perspective* (Dallas: Word, 1990), p. 9.

[9]Tom Smith, *Raw Spirituality* (Downers Grove, IL: IVP Books, 2014), p. 17.

[10]"Systems Theory," *Wikipedia*, http://en.wikipedia.org/wiki/Systems_theory.

[11]We also know this to be true from sexual assault cases. Even though their bodies were used, they have lasting personal and psychological problems associated with the abuse of their bodies.

[12]Stanley Grenz, *Sexual Ethics: A Biblical Perspective* (Dallas: Word, 1990), p. 17.

[13]"Do you not know that your bodies are members of Christ himself? Shall I then take the members of Christ and unite them with a prostitute? Never! Do you not know that he who unites himself with a prostitute is one with her in body? For it is said, 'The two will become one flesh.' But whoever is united with the Lord is one with him in spirit" (1 Cor 6:15-17).

[14]Rowland Croucher, *Still Waters, Deep Waters: Meditations and Prayers for Busy People* (Sutherland, Australia: Albatross Books, 1987), pp. 96-97.

[15]Christopher West, *Theology of the Body for Beginners: A Basic Introduction to Pope John Paul II's Sexual Revolution* (West Chester, PA: Ascension Press, 2004), p. 5.

[16]Ibid., p. 6.

[17]Balswick and Balswick, *Authentic Human Sexuality*, p. 18.

[18]"Sex Drive: How Do Men and Women Compare?" *WebMD*, www.webmd .com/sex/features/sex-drive-how-do-men-women-compare?page=3.

[19]Philip Blumstein and Pepper Swartz, cited in Robbie Gonzalez, "Do Men Really Have Higher Sex Drives Than Women?" *io9*, January 21, 2013, http://io9. com/5977668/do-men-really-have-higher-sex-drives-than-women.

[20]Ibid.

[21]If C. S. Lewis is right in claiming that all our vices are virtues gone wrong, then in order to really understand what is being sought in the sinful action we need to discern the virtue in the vice. What creational good is actually being sought in the wrong place? Another way of looking at this is that we are fixating on one inherently good thing but divorcing it from its overarching creational purpose that gives that good its true meaning. For instance, Alan's way of describing the allure of pornography for the male is "the love of beauty, divorced from the love of goodness, separated from the pain of relationship." Seen in this way, the lustful person is captivated by beauty, but has failed to pursue the broader moral imperatives (goodness) and honor the deeper purposes of sex (relationship) and so find themselves enslaved.

So too when we think of what I have here called social porn; the good being sought in gossip mags and paparazzi trash is probably the desire for relational connection and intimacy, as well as genuine interest in the lives of other people. In its sinful form, however, these good concerns are severed from a guiding sense of righteousness—essentially about right relationships between God, self, others and creation. It is a classic transgression—the spilling over of appropriate boundaries. Without a prevailing love of righteousness we will live our lives through others, objectify people and end up obsessed in an immoderate and unwholesome interest in their personal affairs.

[22]James B. Nelson, "Reuniting Sexuality and Spirituality," *Christian Century*, February 25, 1987, www.religion-online.org/showarticle.asp?title=114.

[23]Frank Vilaasa, *What Is Love? The Spiritual Purpose of Relationships* (Koh Samui, Thailand: Lotus Yoga, 2007), p. 83.

[24]C. S. Lewis, *The Four Loves* (New York: Harcourt Brace, 1960), p. 7.

[25]Joseph Agassi, "Deception: A View from the Rationalist Perspective," in *Mythomanias: The Nature of Deception and Self-Deception*, ed. Michael S. Myslobodsky (Mahwah, NJ: Psychology Press, 1997), p. 25.

[26]Cognitive dissonance—a concept developed in social psychology—helps us understand some of the psychological processes we all go through internally as we navigate some of this tricky stuff. Humans don't like to live with too much internal tension, in other words, we need to have some level of consistency in our belief system, particularly as they match our behaviors (for example, someone who believes in the "no sex before marriage ethic," yet continues to sleep with his or her partner). This inconsistency between what one believes and how one lives creates a level of discomfort or dissonance within the individual to which they must eventually seek some form of resolve. In other words, they will stop the behavior in accordance to their belief, or they will change their belief in order to accommodate the behavior.

[27]Jeff Goldblum and Tom Berenger, in Lawrence Kasdan and Barbara Benedek, *The Big Chill*, directed by Lawrence Kasdan (Culver City, CA: Colombia Pictures, 1983).

[28]Philip Yancey, *Rumors of Another World: What on Earth Are We Missing?* (Grand Rapids: Zondervan, 2003), p. 89.

[29]See "Arranged/Forced Marriage Statistics," *Statistic Brain*, accessed November 14, 2014, www.statisticbrain.com/arranged-marriage-statistics.

[30]Dietrich Bonhoeffer, *The Cost of Discipleship*, trans. R. H. Fuller (New York: Touchstone, 1959), pp. 96-98.

CHAPTER 5: GENDER MATTERS

[1]Jeanne Maglaty, "When Did Girls Start Wearing Pink?" *Smithsonian.com*, April 7, 2011, www.smithsonianmag.com/arts-culture/When-Did-Girls-Start -Wearing-Pink.html#ixzz1sVfJrowZ.

[2]Ibid.

[3]Hilary M. Lips, *Sex and Gender: An Introduction* (Boston: McGraw Hill, 2005), p. 5.

[4]A. H. Devor, "How Many Sexes? How Many Genders? When Two Are Not Enough," University of Victoria, http://web.uvic.ca/~ahdevor/HowMany /HowMany.html.

[5]Some countries are now beginning to recognize the rights of those who don't fit into the two dominant genders (i.e., men or women). Norrie May-Welby from Australia is one such person who is pushing for legal recognition. See Alecia Simmonds, "The World's First Genderless Person," *Stuff.co.nz*, August 11, 2013, www.stuff.co.nz/life-style/life/9378281/The-worlds-first-genderless -person.

[6]"Gender Dysphoria," *PubMed Health*, February 24, 2014, www.ncbi.nlm .nih.gov/pubmedhealth/PMH0002495.

[7]"Gender Identity," *Wikipedia*, http://en.wikipedia.org/wiki/Gender_identity.

[8]Lloyd deMause, "The Evolution of Childrearing," in "The Emotional Life of Nations," Psychohistory.com, www.psychohistory.com/books/the -emotional-life-of-nations/chapter-8-the-evolution-of-child-rearing/.

[9]Stanley Grenz, *Sexual Ethics: A Biblical Perspective* (Dallas: Word, 1990), p. 22.

[10]Ibid., p. 23. Grenz also notes that even in the New Testament, which was written long after Mediterranean society had moved beyond the prehistoric stage, women are referred to as "the weaker partner" (1 Peter 3:7).

[11]There are people who do have sex reassignment surgery—they can from all outward appearances change their sex. However they still remain genetically the sex they were born with.

[12]Philomena D'Souza, *Woman: Icon of Liberation* (Bombay: Better Yourself, 2005), p. 72, http://books.google.com/books?id=-oHLLGUFwhMC&pg =PA72&source=gbs_selected_pages&cad=3#v=onepage&q&f=false.

[13]Tim M. Kellis, review of *Men Are from Mars, Women Are from Venus,* by John Gray, AuthorsDen.com, January 30, 2009, www.authorsden.com /visit/viewarticle.asp?id=45674.

[14]Dorothy Sayers, cited in Mary Stewart Van Leeuwen, *My Brother's Keeper: What the Social Sciences Do (and Don't) Tell Us About Masculinity* (Downers Grove, IL: IVP Academic, 2002), p. 28.

[15]Van Leeuwen, *My Brother's Keeper,* p. 32.

[16]Ibid.

[17]Ibid., p. 89.

[18]David Mattingly and Eric Marrapodi, "Pastor Who Sparked Outrage Over Hitting Gay Children Speaks Out," CNN, May 8, 2012, http://religion .blogs.cnn.com/2012/05/08/pastor-who-sparked-outrage-over-hitting -gay-children-speaks-out.

[19]"Transsexual," *Urban Dictionary*, www.urbandictionary.com/define.php? term=transsexual.

[20]Michael Frost, *Longing for Love: Gender, Sexuality and our Experience of God* (Sutherland, Australia: Albatross Books, 1996), p. 199.

[21]Ibid., p. 197.

[22]Dorothy Sayers, quoted in ibid., p. 202.

[23]Tony Campolo, "Embracing the Feminine Side of God," *Red Letter Christians,*

February 9, 2011, www.redletterchristians.org/embracing-the-feminine
-side-of-god.

CHAPTER 6: BI NOW, GAY LATER?

[1]Peter Frampton, "I'm in You," *I'm in You*, Universal, 1977.
[2]Engaging in homosexual behavior because there is no possibility of heterosexual engagement is typically called "situational homosexuality."
[3]"Kinsey's Heterosexual-Homosexual Scale," Kinsey Institute, accessed September 30, 2014, www.kinseyinstitute.org/resources/ak-hhscale.html.
[4]Ibid.
[5]"The BSPI: Beiter Sexual Preference Indicator," *Beiter Sexual Preference Indicator*, accessed September 30, 2014, www.bspitest.com/tests.html; "Klein
Sexual Orientation Grid," *Wikipedia*, accessed September 30, 2014, http://
en.wikipedia.org/wiki/Klein_Sexual_Orientation_Grid; Robert Epstein;
"Straight, Gay, or in Between?" *MySexualOrientation.com*, accessed September
30, 2014, http://mysexualorientation.com; Ben Roe, "A Sexual Orientation
Worksheet," *Tuxwheels Communications*, accessed September 30, 2014, http://
jbenjaminroe.com/writings/kleingrid.html.
[6]*Baker Encyclopedia of Psychology*, ed. David G. Benner (Grand Rapids: Baker,
1985), pp. 520-26.
[7]Cathy Renna, "Cynthia Nixon's Only Real Choice? Honesty," *Huffington Post*,
January 25, 2012, www.huffingtonpost.com/cath-renna/cynthia-nixon
-choice_b_1231025.html.
[8]Roy F. Baumeister, "Gender Differences in Erotic Plasticity: The Female Sex
Drive as Socially Flexible and Responsive," *Psychological Bulletin 126*, no. 3
(May 2000), http://psycnet.apa.org/index.cfm?fa=buy.optionToBuy&id
=2000-15386-001. "Men are very rigid and specific about who they become
aroused by, who they want to have sex with, who they fall in love with," says
J. Michael Bailey, a Northwestern University sex researcher and coauthor with
Meredith Chivers on the study. By contrast, women may be more open to
same-sex *relationships* thanks to their less-directed sex drives, Bailey says.
"Women probably have the capacity to become sexually interested in and fall
in love with their own sex more than men do," Bailey says. "They won't necessarily do it, but they have the capacity." Bailey's contention is backed up by
studies showing that homosexuality is a more fluid state among women than
men. In another broad review of studies, Baumeister found many more lesbians reported recent sex with men when compared to gay men's reports of
sex with women. Women were also more likely than men to call themselves
bisexual and to report their sexual orientation as a matter of choice ("Sex Drive:
How Do Men and Women Compare?" *WebMD*, accessed September 30, 2014,
www.webmd.com/sex/features/sex-drive-how-do-men-women-
compare?page=3).
[9]Katy Perry, "I Kissed a Girl," *One of the Boys*, EMI, 2008.

[10]Jenell Williams Paris, *The End of Sexual Identity: Why Sex Is Too Important to Define Who We Are* (Downers Grove, IL: IVP Books, 2011), p. 31.
[11]Ibid., p. 51.
[12]"Sexual Orientation and Homosexuality," American Psychological Association, accessed October 1, 2014, www.apa.org/topics/sexuality/orientation.aspx.
[13]Tracy Baim, "In Defense of Cynthia Nixon: Why 'Born This Way' Doesn't Matter," *Huffington Post*, January 23, 2012, www.huffingtonpost.com/tracy -baim/cynthia-nixon-choice_b_1224241.html.

CHAPTER 7: LIMPING STRAIGHT TO HEAVEN

[1]*Exclusive*, meaning they have *never* experienced heterosexual response, to becoming exclusively heterosexual, meaning they *no longer* have any homosexual response.
[2]C. S. Lewis, *The Allegory of Love*, 2nd ed. (Oxford: Oxford University Press, 1969), p. 1.
[3]Gerald May, *Addiction and Grace: Love and Spirituality in the Healing of Addictions* (New York: HarperOne, 1988), p. 78.
[4]Ed Payne, "Group Apologizes to Gay Community, Shuts Down 'Cure' Ministry," *CNN.com*, July 8, 2013, www.cnn.com/2013/06/20/us/exodus -international-shutdown.
[5]Many ministries have evolved over time and no longer hold to such ideals.
[6]Wendy Vanderwal-Gritter, *Generous Spaciousness: Responding to Gay Christians in the Church* (Grand Rapids: Brazos, 2014), p. 111.
[7]Howard A. Snyder, *Homosexuality and the Church: Defining Issue or Distracting Battle?* (Wilmore, KY: Seedbed, 2014), pp. 15-16.
[8]Vanderwal-Gritter, *Generous Spaciousness*, p. 106.

CHAPTER 8: UNCOMFORTABLE SEX POSITIONS

[1]Ed Stetzer, cited in Alan Hirsch and Debra Hirsch, *Untamed: Reactivating a Missional Form of Discipleship* (Grand Rapids: Baker, 2012), p. 222.
[2]It's interesting to note that this widening generational gap is seen (statistically) on a number of ethical issues, not just the gay one. See for example, Dan Merica, "Survey: Young Christians Want Marijuana Legalized," CNN, April 25, 2013, http://religion.blogs.cnn.com/2013/04/25/survey-young-christians -want-marijuana-legalized/?utm_source=buffer&utm_medium =twitter&utm _campaign=Buffer:+chadrallen+on+twitter&buffer_share =0227c.
[3]See the Human Rights Campaign website at www.hrc.org; see also "California Proposition 8 (2008)," *Wikipedia*, http://en.wikipedia.org/wiki/California _Proposition_8.
[4]Gregory A. Boyd, *Repenting of Religion: Turning from Judgment to the Love of God* (Grand Rapids: Baker, 2004), p. 89.
[5]See Ted Grimsrud, "The 'Homosexuality' Debate: Two Streams of Biblical Interpretation," *Peace Theology*, accessed September 30, 2014, http://peacetheology.

net/homosexuality/the-homosexuality-debate-two-streams-of-biblical
-interpretation; and Dan O. Via and Robert A. J. Gagnon, *Homosexuality and the
Bible: Two Views* (Minneapolis: Fortress Press, 2003).
[6]The Wesleyan Quadrilateral was developed by Albert C. Outler in the twentieth
century to help us understand the sources John Wesley drew upon in his theology and ministry. See Don Thorsen, *The Wesleyan Quadrilateral: A Model of
Evangelical Theology* (Lexington, KY: Emeth Press, 2005). Howard Snyder
(among others) has suggested a reworking of the Quadrilateral to a Pentalateral,
to include Wesley's emphasis on the created order. See http://howardsnyder.
seedbed.com/2014/05/24/the-radicaler-wesley/.
[7]With the Wesleyan Quadrilateral, the work and guidance of the Holy Spirit is
presumed to be crucial. Wesley himself acknowledged the unique role that
the Holy Spirit plays in helping us come to theological truth. The Spirit first
inspired the writing of the Scriptures and continues to inspire and guide us
as we seek to interpret them, our history and personal experience. Let's look
briefly at each pillar.
Scripture. The Scriptures hold the prime place when discerning the will of
God. "It's the unique testimony to God's self-disclosure in the life of Israel; in
the ministry, death and resurrection of Jesus the Christ; and in the Spirit's work
in the early church." The Bible *must* be our primary source when struggling to
discern the will of God. We all need to grapple with the text, both in understanding its original context and its applicability in our own lives and context.
Tradition. As God's people we don't have to work out things alone, we have a
rich tradition with many saints and heroes of the faith who have gone before
us. Many have wrestled with exactly the same things we do. We can and must
learn from both the truths and the mistakes they made. And this also includes
what we learn from God's people today. Believing that God continues to speak
to his people, we submit ourselves to the broader community of faith for accountability, prayer and discernment.
Experience. A third source and criterion of our theology is our personal experience. I love the way experience is described by the Wesleyans themselves:
"By experience we mean especially the 'new life in Christ,' which is ours as a
gift of God's grace; such rebirth and personal assurance gives us new eyes to
see the living truth in Scripture. But we mean also the broader experience of
all the life we live, its joys, its hurts, its yearnings. So we interpret the Bible in
light of our cumulative experiences. We interpret our life's experience in light
of the biblical message. We do so not only for our experience individually but
also for the experience of the whole human family."
Reason. Faith and reason are often seen as at odds with one another, although
they actually need each other. Without reason one can't possibly fully understand the truths of revelation. God has created us as *reason*able beings, and
part of our intellectual capacity is to be able to comprehend and discover
God's truths. But again, our reason is to be guided by the Spirit. "We use it

(reason) in relating the Scripture and tradition to our experience and in organizing our theological witness in a way that's internally coherent." See *United Methodist Member's Handbook*, rev. George Koehler (Nashville: Discipleship Resources, 2006), pp. 64-65.

[8]William J. Webb, *Slaves, Women and Homosexuals: Exploring the Hermeneutics of Cultural Analysis* (Downers Grove, IL: IVP Academic, 2001).

[9]Daniel B. Wallace, "As Easy as X-Y-Z: A Review of William Webb's 'Slaves, Women and Homosexuals,'" Bible.org, accessed September 30, 2014, https://bible.org/article/easy-x-y-z-review-william-webbs-slaves-women-and-homosexuals.

[10]Webb, *Slaves, Women and Homosexuals*, p. 32.

[11]Ibid., p. 40. Under the Z in figure 8.3 Webb adds "utilization of a sliding scale of culpability, and variation in the degree of negative assessment based on the type of same-sex activity." Webb appreciates the variety of nuance and what he calls a multilevel ethic.

[12]Ibid., p. 40.

[13]Walter Brueggemann, "The Third World of Evangelical Imagination," in *Interpretation and Obedience: From Faithful Reading to Faithful Living* (Minneapolis: Fortress Press, 1991), p. 26 n. 18.

[14]Based on the Great Commission, where Jesus calls us to disciple the nations, our missional engagement should be based on discipling *all* people, not just Christians. Now this will look different from believers to not-yet believers, but in all our relationships we can call people toward the greater ideals of the kingdom, hoping that as they live into them they will see and experience the God of the kingdom. In both *Untamed* (the book Alan and I coauthored) and Alan's ebook on *Disciplism*, we talk about the concept of pre- and postconversion discipleship. See either publication for a more expanded understanding.

CHAPTER 9: THE BENT SCAPEGOAT

[1]Richard Beck, *Unclean: Meditations on Purity, Hospitality, and Mortality* (Eugene, OR: Wipf & Stock, 2011), p. 7.

[2]For an interesting study done on sterilizing cockroaches, see Michael D. Lemonick, "Why We Get Disgusted," *Time.com*, May 24, 2007, www.time.com/time/magazine/article/0,9171,1625167,00.html.

[3]Beck, *Unclean*, p. 2.

[4]Ibid., p. 8.

[5]Ibid., p. 9.

[6]Mark Labberton, *The Dangerous Act of Loving Your Neighbor* (Downers Grove, IL: IVP Books, 2010), p. 23.

[7]Ibid., p. 50.

[8]"Homosexuality, Stigma, and Biocultural Evolution," *Journal of Gay and Lesbian Psychotherapy* 1, no. 4 (1991), www.tandfonline.com/doi/abs/10.1300/j236v01n04_02#.VFPkyksgvZo.

[9]I'm not suggesting we do away with all categorization. Clearly categories of normal and deviant are needed to assess certain standards. For example, the social sciences develop norms as it relates to behavior and general functioning, assessments need to be made about what is and isn't deficient, needs improvement, and so forth.

[10]It's interesting that heterosexuality, the norm, as a construct, did not exist prior to the conception of homosexuality. See Ladelle McWhorter, "Foucault's Genealogy of Homosexuality," *Journal of French and Francophone Philosophy* 6, nos. 1-2 (1994), http://web.ics.purdue.edu/~smith132/French_Philosophy /Sp94/fouca.pdf.

[11]Erving Goffman, *Stigma: Notes on the Management of Spoiled Identity* (New York: Touchstone, 1986), p. 5.

[12]"Suicide Among LGBT Youth," *Wikipedia*, accessed October 1, 2014, http:// en.wikipedia.org/wiki/Suicide_among_LGBT_youth.

[13]H. E. Adams, L. W. Wright Jr., and B. A. Lohr, "Is Homophobia Associated with Homosexual Arousal?" *Journal of Abnormal Psychology* 105, no. 3 (August 1996): 440-45. Abstract: "The authors investigated the role of homosexual arousal in exclusively heterosexual men who admitted negative affect toward homosexual individuals. Participants consisted of a group of homophobic men (n = 35) and a group of nonhomophobic men (n = 29); they were assigned to groups on the basis of their scores on the Index of Homophobia (W. W. Hudson & W. A. Ricketts, 1980). The men were exposed to sexually explicit erotic stimuli consisting of heterosexual, male homosexual, and lesbian videotapes, and changes in penile circumference were monitored. They also completed an Aggression Questionnaire (A. H. Buss & M. Perry, 1992). Both groups exhibited increases in penile circumference to the heterosexual and female homosexual videos. Only the homophobic men showed an increase in penile erection to male homosexual stimuli. The groups did not differ in aggression. Homophobia is apparently associated with homosexual arousal that the homophobic individual is either unaware of or denies."

[14]"Study Finds Homophobes Fear Their Parents, Repress Sexuality," Gay News Network, updated April 11, 2011, http://gaynewsnetwork.com.au/news /study-finds-homophobes-fear-their-parents-repress-sexuality-5862.html.

[15]Letha Dawson Scanzoni and Virginia Ramey Mollenkott, *Is the Homosexual My Neighbor? A Positive Christian Response* (San Francisco: Harper, 1994), p. 28.

[16]Gordon Allport, *The Nature of Prejudice* (Reading, MA: Addison Wesley, 1954), pp. 9-10.

[17]Scanzoni and Mollenkott, *Is the Homosexual My Neighbor?*, p. 46.

CHAPTER 10: IMAGO GAY

[1]Dietrich Bonhoeffer, *Life Together* (San Francisco: HarperCollins, 1954), p. 93.

[2]Alan Hirsch and Debra Hirsch, *Untamed: Reactivating a Missional Form of Discipleship* (Grand Rapids: Baker, 2010), p. 242.

³Ibid., p. 243.

⁴*The Works of the Reverend William Law*, vol. IV (London: privately reprinted for G. Moreton, 1893), p. 228.

⁵Stephen Covey, *The 7 Habits of Highly Effective People: Powerful Lessons in Personal Change* (New York: Simon and Schuster, 2004), p. 267.

⁶Flannery O'Connor, "The Fiction Writer and His Country," in *Mystery and Manners* (New York: Farrar, Straus and Giroux, 1961), p. 34.

⁷Jean Vanier, *Community and Growth: Our Pilgrimage Together* (New York: Paulist Press, 1979), p. 155.

⁸See 100Revs's website at www.100revs.net.

⁹The Marin Foundation has undertaken a similar campaign associated with annual gay pride parades throughout the United States.

¹⁰Elton John, "Sorry Seems to Be the Hardest Word," *Blue Moves*, MCAS, 1976.

CHAPTER 11: RE-SEXING THE CHURCH

¹Alan Hirsch and Debra Hirsch, *Untamed: Reactivating a Missional Form of Discipleship* (Grand Rapids: Baker, 2010), p. 157.

²Ibid., p. 173.

³See "Families and Living Arrangements: 2013," United States Census Bureau, accessed October 2, 2014, www.census.gov/hhes/families/data/cps2013 .html?eml=gd&utm_medium=email&utm_source=govdelivery.

⁴Emily Babay, "Census: Big Decline in Nuclear Family," *Philly.com*, November 26, 2013, www.philly.com/philly/news/How_American_families_are _changing.html

⁵See Rodney Clapp, *Families at the Crossroads: Beyond Tradition and Modern Options* (Downers Grove, IL: IVP Books, 1993).

⁶Stanley Hauerwas, *Matthew*, Brazos Theological Commentary (Grand Rapids: Brazos, 2006), p. 125.

⁷Ibid.

⁸Janet Fishburne, quoted in Hirsch and Hirsch, *Untamed*, p. 168.

⁹Wesley Hill, quoted in Allison J. Althoff, "Hope for the Gay Undergrad," *Christianity Today*, December 7, 2012, www.christianitytoday.com/ct/2013/january-february/hope-for-gay-undergrad.html?utm_source=ctweekly-html&utm _medium=Newsletter&utm_term=12331065&utm_content=149872808&utm _campaign=2013&start=4.

¹⁰Nelson Mandela, cited in Hirsch and Hirsch, *Untamed*, p. 171.

¹¹Lesslie Newbigin, *The Gospel in a Pluralist Society* (Grand Rapids: Eerdmans, 1989), p. 227.

¹²Social set theory was developed to observe the relationship between groups of people and their social environments, looking specifically at the structures that any given group organizes around. They describe three basic models that most organizations or groups fall into: the bounded set, the centered set and fuzzy sets. The two that I want to look at in relation to the church are the *bounded*

Missio Alliance

and

≋ InterVarsity Press

Missio Alliance has arisen in response to the shared voice of pastors and ministry leaders from across the landscape of North American Christianity for a new "space" of togetherness and reflection amid the issues and challenges facing the church in our day. We are united by a desire for a fresh expression of evangelical faith, one significantly informed by the global evangelical family. Lausanne's Cape Town Commitment, "A Confession of Faith and a Call to Action," provides an excellent guidepost for our ethos and aims.

In partnership with InterVarsity Press, we are pleased to offer a line of resources authored by a diverse range of theological practitioners. The resources in this series are selected based on the important way in which they address and embody these values, and thus, the unique contribution they offer in equipping Christian leaders for fuller and more faithful participation in God's mission.

Available Titles

The Church as Movement by JR Woodward and Dan White Jr., 978-0-8308-4133-2

Emboldened by Tara Beth Leach, 978-0-8308-4524-8

Embrace by Leroy Barber, 978-0-8308-4471-5

Faithful Presence by David E. Fitch, 978-0-8308-4127-1

God Is Stranger by Krish Kandiah, 978-0-8308-4532-3

Paradoxology by Krish Kandiah, 978-0-8308-4504-0

Redeeming Sex by Debra Hirsch, 978-0-8308-3639-0

Seven Practices for the Church on Mission by David E. Fitch, 978-0-8308-4142-4

White Awake by Daniel Hill, 978-0-8308-4393-0

missioalliance.org | twitter.com/missioalliance | facebook.com/missioalliance and *centered* sets. See Michael Frost and Alan Hirsch, *The Shaping of Things to Come: Mission and Innovation for the 21st Century Church* (Grand Rapids: Baker, 2013), pp. 68-72, 252-54.

[13]See Alan Hirsch's ebook *Disciplism: Reimagining Evangelism Through the Lens of Discipleship* (Centreville, VA: Exponential Resources, 2014) for a comprehensive look at how evangelism is reframed through the lens of discipleship and not the other way around.

[14]Jack W. Niewold, "Set Theory and Leadership: Reflections on Missional Communities in the Light of Ephesians 4:11-12," *Journal of Biblical Perspectives in Leadership* 2, no. 1 (Winter 2008), www.regent.edu/acad/global/publications /jbpl/vol2no1/Niewold_Jack_Final.pdf. To see how we did this while leading our complex community in Melbourne, see Frost and Hirsch, *Shaping of Things to Come*, pp. 252-54, and Hirsch and Hirsch, *Untamed*, pp. 151-55.

[15]Gregory A. Boyd, *Repenting of Religion* (Grand Rapids: Baker, 2004), p. 46.

[16]See David Fitch and Geoff Holsclaw, *Prodigal Christianity: 10 Signposts into the Missional Frontier* (San Francisco: Jossey-Bass, 2013).

[17]To see pictures of the "Church Lady" from *Saturday Night Live*, go to http:// goo.gl/NmkxSD.

[18]Tullian Tchividjian, "God's Word in Two Words," *Christianity Today*, August 29, 2013, www.christianitytoday.com/ct/2013/september/law-gospel-gods -word-in-two-words.html?start=2.

[19]Max Lucado, cited in "Discipleship Is Messy," *Christianity Today*, January 17, 2013, www.christianitytoday.com/ct/2013/january-february/discipleship-is -messy.html?utm_source=ctweekly-html&utm_medium=Newsletter&utm _term=12331065&utm_content=149872808&utm_campaign=2013&start=1.

CONCLUSION: THE CLIMAX

[1]John L. Mood and Rainer Maria Rilke, *Rilke on Love and Other Difficulties: Translations and Considerations* (New York: W. W. Norton, 1975), p. 32.

[2]"The Life of Sigmund Freud," PBS.org, accessed October 2, 2014, www.pbs .org/wgbh/questionofgod/twolives/freudbio.html.